HERBS IN COOKING
Dietary choices
from nature's supply
of seasonings and drugs

Translation: **Maria Bitsakaki**

Photography: **Nikos Psilakis**

Lay-out: **Nikos Dretakis**

Printing: **TYPOKRETA**
Industrial area, Heraklion
Tel.: 0810 380882

Bookbinding: **Z. Moudatsakis**
Skoteino, Heraklion

ISBN: 960-7448-29-4

KARMANOR

Lophos Semeli
71500 Heraklion
Crete, Greece
Tel. & Fax: 0030 810 261920
E-mail: npsilakis@otenet.gr

MARIA & NIKOS PSILAKIS

Herbs
IN COOKING

*Dietary choices from nature's supply
of seasonings and drugs*

with 255 recipes

KARMANOR

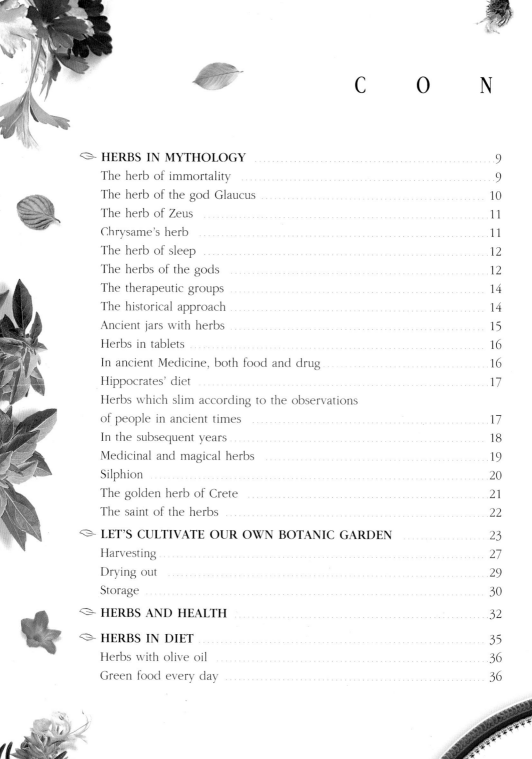

C O N T

N T S

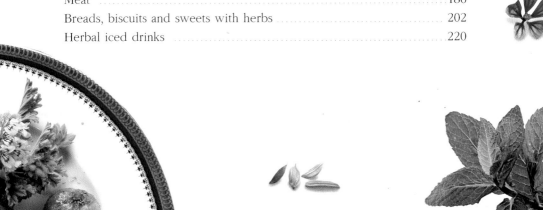

INTRODUCTION

*If people ate correctly and ate
well then there would not be any illnesses!*

(Hippocrates, De prisca medicina, 3)

It has been 2.500 years since the father of the medical science first acknowledged the relation of nutrition with health! That relation had been suggested by Homer a few centuries before then. A lot of things have changed since ancient times, the science itself has changed, however Hippocrates' statement has always been ahead of the times. Contemporary Medicine has turned to the Mediterranean and especially to Crete and other Greek areas, because it has been found that in these regions heart diseases were almost unknown and cancer incidences were much fewer than in other areas that were studied, as long as the people kept to the traditional dietary habits.

What indeed is this dietary model? It is the development of an ancient nutritional inheritance that is based on nature and has the following basic characteristics:

❖ Consumption of plenty of fruits, greens and vegetables (every day).

❖ Fish: once or twice a week.

❖ Meat: once a week.

❖ Olive oil: the only fat substance consumed on a daily basis!

❖ Frequent consumption of pulses and wine (one glass with each meal).

People in the Mediterranean have looked to nature from ancient times, not only for food but also for their medicines. The study of medicinal herbs started in antiquity. Hundreds of herbs have been studied since then and have taught people valuable lessons for life. Looking for medicines in the pharmaceutical wealth of nature has been a common characteristic for many cultures, all over the world. In ancient Greece the same plants were used both as food and as medicine. The doctors had realized that the appropriate diet could not only prevent but also cure certain diseases! It is recorded that Pothalirius, the son of Aesculapius, the god of Medicine, cured

people with proper nutrition, unlike his brother, Machaon, who was a surgeon. The way Hippocrates writes about this therapeutic diet shows that it was highly recommended by the doctors of that time. Galenus, a great physician in the Roman times, split the therapeutic side of Medicine into three areas. One of them was diet. The other two were surgery and pharmaceutics.

Nevertheless, it was Hippocrates, the father of Medicine, who first taught that food should not only be healthy but also tasty. That wise physician had realized how important it was for people to feel pleased with food and taught the value of moderation in gastronomy:

Engraving by A. Tassos.

"Consume pleasant foods and drinks even if they are not of great quality. You should prefer these, than foods which are of very good quality but are not pleasant in taste"!

In addition, he advised using a lot of aromatic herbs in cooking, so that one could satisfy one's hunger with a little food, because overeating is not good for the health!

This book has tried to keep with Hippocrates' recommendations. It is based on the Greek traditional diet, which is a development of the ancient Greek model, using ingredients from the "pharmacy of nature" and presents beverages, dishes and preparations that are pleasant to the taste and scented with the amazing flavours offered by herbs. It is certainly the result of a quest into the infinite possibilities of nature and has both a practical and cultural content.

We searched the contribution of the plant world to the creation of the dietary patterns of the Mediterranean people, but also the historical and cultural frame surrounding them.

We tried to learn from the experience of former generations. We selected the commonest herbs of the Greek and the general Mediterranean regions and present them in a brief but concise way, giving their botanic description (how to recognize them) but also historical and cultural information, their application in ancient Medicine, as well as their use in contemporary cooking... In addition, 255 representative recipes are included, which can help in getting acquainted with the use of herbs in cooking. Besides being beneficial for health, they can offer amazing flavours and inspiration for gastronomic creations!

Dry measures
1 cup flour= *150 grams*
1 cup semolina or caster sugar = *130 grams*
1 cup sugar = *230 grams*
1 cup rice = *230 grams*
1 cup grated cheese = *100 grams*
1 cup chopped almonds or walnuts = *100 grams*

Liquids
1 cup = *225 ml*
1 cup = *16 tablespoons (tbsp)*
1 tablespoon = *3 teaspoons*
1 tablespoon = *15 ml*
1 teaspoon = *5 ml*

ACKNOWLEDGEMENTS...

The study of the vast world of greens and herbs was based on the knowledge we have gained since childhood, having grown up in two regions of the island with experience and traditions of thousands of years! The older generations, who had relied upon nature for their survival (among them our parents), are the best teachers of all of us. We thank them, together with the people who guided us into their gastronomic traditions, on Crete, the Peloponnese (an area where herbs are abundantly used in cooking), Northern Greece, the islands...
Special thanks we owe to:

• Dr Zach. Kypriotakis, teacher at the TEI of Crete, with vast experience which has been completed with the competence of the scientist, the botanist who has made his hobby his profession. It is to him that we owe the description and classification of the herbs that are included in this book.

• Melanie Goodwin for her help in the translation into English.

• Evangelia Strataki, teacher of English at the School of Agriculture, TEI of Crete, for her help with the agricultural terminology.

• Our friends from Cyprus, Corsica, Moroco, Sicily, Tunisia, France and Spain who, whenever necessary, gave us information both oral and written! Among them are: Kostas Kokkinoftas, Mireille Jourdane, Djavad Mossalayi.

• We also thank all our friends from various Greek regions who guided us into their local gastronomic traditions.

HERBS IN
mythology

⤳ The herb of immortality

It may give life, eternal beauty or immortality itself! Behind every miraculous event, there may be a herb... The history of civilisation is full of myths and legends which refer to the medicinal use of plants. Among all these stories there is one herb which stands out; one that was known only by a few and was rarely used: the herb of immortality! Whether it is known as "molly" or maybe "aeizoon" (everlasting life) does not really matter. What counts is that this herb is not easily found. It was only known to the gods and a few mortals who had found out about it by accident most probably.

The name Glaucus stands out in mythology. He was known as the son of the legendary king of Crete, Minos, and also as the god of the sea who was notorious for his affairs. The common factor which links these two mythical characters with the name Glaucus, is one herb. One of them (the son of Minos) was brought back to life with the herb and the other Glaucus used it to become immortal!

Could it be that this was one and the same herb?

Minos' son was young when he got lost in the palace at Knossos. He was looked for everywhere within the royal residence but could be found nowhere. After searching for a long time, a famous seer, Polyidus, was asked to help. On observing the flight of some birds, he was able to find the boy in the royal storerooms. He had fallen into a large urn storing honey and had drowned! Minos determined that such a wise seer as Polyidus could not only find Glaucus but also bring him back to life! Polyidus was terrified to think that he was obliged to resurrect the boy, but the king insisted.

Polyidus was buried along with the dead second snake came into the tomb, but on seeing the other dead reptile, turned around and left through the hole, only to return with a herb in its mouth. The dead snake was touched by this herb and immediately came back to life. Without losing a moment, Polyidus took the herb and placed it on Glaucus' body. The corpse started to move and the young boy was resurrected!

Many years passed by and people, who had heard of this amazing story, hoped to find

Glaucus is no longer dead! He has been resurrected with the herb that the snake brought into the grave! Polyidus is opposite him (cylix of 5th c. B.C.).

young Glaucus on the day when the tomb was closed, as there he would be able to think more clearly and so bring the young boy back to life. For a while he was desperate until he saw a small hole in the tomb through which a snake made its way in. The reptile slowly slithered along until it was in front of the corpse of the young boy. Polyidus was petrified that the snake might do harm to the boy's body and so he picked up a stone and killed it! Shortly afterwards a the same herb. Unfortunately, Polyidus was the first and the last who found (most probably by accident) this miraculous herb.

⌒ The herb of the god Glaucus

Also during that time, back in the days of mythology, there was another Glaucus who happened to link his fate with a herb. He was a simple fisherman. One day he

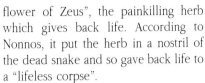

found a strange fish in his net which was already half dead from its efforts to escape and was fighting a losing battle. Suddenly it managed to bite a herb. It immediately came back to life and jumped back into the sea. Intrigued by what he had seen, Glaucus did the same and so he tried the herb. He felt his powers getting stronger and then he dived into the water, full of life. From that point, Glaucus ceased to be a fisherman. The herb which he had eaten had made him immortal. Sea nymphs rushed towards him to release him from every mortal tie and from then on he travelled without rest through the seas, helping sailors and his old companions, the fishermen.

The miraculous herb had worked its miracle. However, it gave eternal life, but not eternal youth. With the passing of each day Glaucus the Anthedonian (he had been born in Anthedon) grew older and older. He was the oldest immortal in Greek mythology!

The herb of Zeus

Nonnos, a poet in the 5th century A.D., describes with amazing detail the resurrection of a hero in Greek mythology with "the flower of Zeus". The hero was known as Tyllos or Tyllon and he died from the bite of a poisonous snake. The reptile had coiled itself up on the hero's body and tapped him three times with its tail and then bitten him on the face. Moria, Tyllon's sister had watched this terrifying scene and had rushed for help from the giant Damacene, a huge son of Zeus.

Damacene rushed to the scene and killed the snake but Tyllon was already dead. Shortly afterwards, another snake appeared, a female one, probably the other one's mate. It quickly went to a rock and broke off a herb with its jaw, "the

flower of Zeus", the painkilling herb which gives back life. According to Nonnos, it put the herb in a nostril of the dead snake and so gave back life to a "lifeless corpse".

Nonnos' detailed description tells us that the dead snake started to move, its body began to tremble and then shake. Some parts of its body did not come back to life straight away, whereas others were immediately resurrected. Firstly its tail began to move slightly and then it started to breathe again. As its throat slowly came back to life, a slight hissing sound could be heard until it reached its normal pitch. Soon the snake began to move and then quickly left, through its secret hole.

Without losing a moment, Moria took the same herb, "the herb of Zeus", the medicine which gives back life and heals pains, and she placed it in one of Tyllon's nostrils. His soul re-entered his body and the flickering flame of life within him started to burn brighter and warm the rest of his body which, until that point, had been the corpse of Tyllon. Life triumphed again over death!

Chrysame's herb

Among the herbs in mythology, "the herb of Chrysame" should be specially mentioned, for this was the herb which brought on craziness!

In a battle, Chrysame decorated a bull by painting its horns gold and fed him on the herb which induces craziness pretending that she was preparing the beast so as to sacrifice it on the altar. Unfortunately the bull got away and went over to the enemy's camp. The enemy, who believed this to be a good omen, sacrificed the beast to the gods and ate its meat. They all went crazy!

(Polyaenus, Strategemata, 8,43)

⇌ The herb of sleep

The Minoans, the creators of the wonderful prehistoric civilisation on Crete (2100-1450 B.C.), depicted one of their goddesses with capsules (heads) of the opium poppy on her head. A little later, in classical Greece, the statues of Demeter, the goddess of crops and fruits, depicted her, too, with poppy capsules in her hands. The bread of worship which was dedicated to

way of inducing sleep but doctors used it as an anaesthetic. Legends echo the use of this herb. As it could bring on anaesthesia, doctors in ancient times used it as a medicine for many illnesses; something like a cure-all!

⇌ The herbs of the Gods

Flowers and plants grew out of the spilt blood of mythical heroes who in ancient times could have been gods themselves.

Daphne's transfiguration into a tree. The first branches have started to grow from her legs. Apollo, the god who had fallen in love with her, is beside her. (A mosaic of the Roman times from Paphos in Cyprus). Below: Narcissus is being transformed into a flower (engraving by A. Tassos, on a Greek stamp from 1958).

this goddess was sealed with the capsule of the Opium poppy. (This is still practised by islanders in the Aegean who dedicate bread to the Virgin Mother)! Legend states that Pluto, the god of Hades, the underworld, had abducted Demeter's daughter. From that time, Persephone lived half the year in the dark palaces of Hades and the other half in the world. Pluto was the god of eternal sleep and the poppy is the herb which induces sleep! Not only was this herb a

Hyacinthus, friend of Apollo, died at a very young age. A flower which took his name grew out of his blood. As Hyacinthus was relatively still a child, it was believed that the flower helped teenagers who took it systematically. It was an elixir of youth. It was for this reason that in ancient times slave traders gave this herb of Hyacinthus to their slaves so as to keep them young for as long as possible.

Right: Herbs and greens are abundant in spring. It is the ideal time for our botanic expeditions.

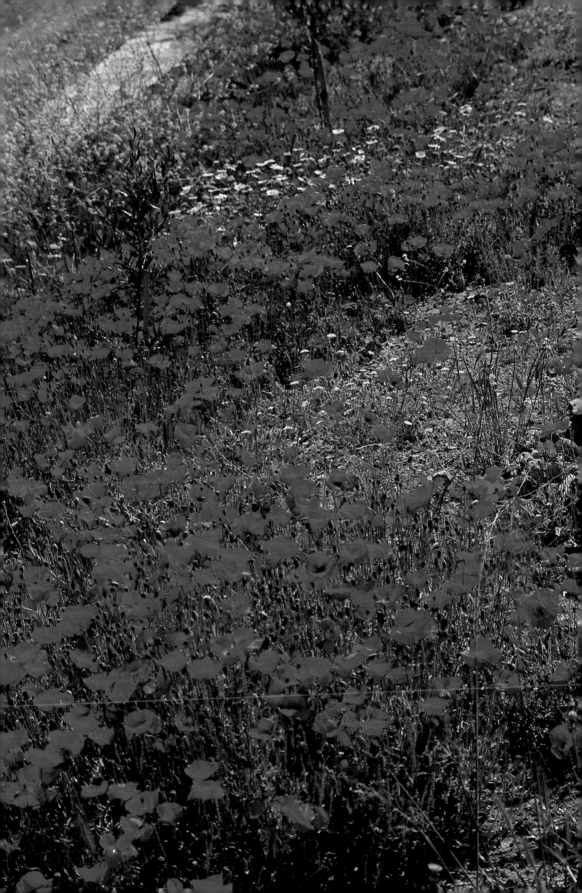

From Prometheus' blood, the hero who stole fire from the gods and managed to give it to man, a magical herb flourished, the crocus of Caucasus. It was Prometheus who was thought to be the great benefactor of mankind. In ancient times he was thought to have taught man how to use herbs for medicinal purposes.

However it was a centaur, Cheiron, who was believed to have the greatest knowledge of herbs. This mythical form of a healer who was half horse, half man, determined the use of herbs as therapies in the ancient world. Herbs such as "centaury" and "cheironion" are strong reminders of his influence in this field.

⤳ The therapeutic groups

The knowledge of herbs and their uses put a great deal of power in the hands of the healers in ancient times. It seems that even so long ago, there were special groupings of therapists that practised some of the most difficult professions. The Idaean Dactyls, a group of metal workers who worked on the mountain of Ida on Crete or in Phrygia are a characteristic example. One of the Idaean Dactyls was called Iasius (he who heals) and another was known as Akesidis. "Akesis" is the therapy and "akeuma" is the medicine. Even up until quite recent times, the practices of these therapeutic methods were kept alive and usually took place in caves, in the country areas. In a Cretan cave, in Arkalochori, metal was found which was intended for procession, showing the use of this particular cave. It was in this same cave that up until a few decades prior to this discovery, women went to give birth.

A fresco from the island of Santorini. A young girl, dressed in colourful clothes, is picking crocuses!

⤳ The historical approach

The history of herbs seems to have begun at the same time as the history of civilisation! In prehistoric Egypt, not only native aromatic plants were used but also herbs from other areas were imported. In a holy papyrus from the beginning of the 18th dynasty (1580-1335 B.C.) therapeutic herbs imported from Crete are mentioned. In general, herbs from Crete were exported to Egypt and the Middle East. On the other hand, herbs from these areas were brought to Crete. The herb trade seems to have had an important role in social interactions which took place in the lower half of the eastern Mediterranean during the Copper Age.

(Source: Chr. Doumas, The frescoes of Thera, Athens 1992).

ARCHAEOLOGICAL AND HISTORICAL EVIDENCE

❧ Ancient jars with herbs!

The excavations at the royal house in Archanes in 2000 by John and Efi Sakellarakis uncovered an important discovery. The royal building had been destroyed in a blaze. The material which had fallen over

From the excavations at the town of Archanes, Crete, by the Sakellarakis couple (summer 2000). Carbonized herbs were found inside large jars, preserved there for 3500 years.
Below: Carbonized herbs from the same excavation.

From that point long ago, the Mediterranean became a sea of interaction and trade. Each civilisation influenced the others in their turn and so the development of Medicine came about, based on the experiences of neighbouring civilisations. It is assumed that the same thing happened with cooking, but there is not enough information at hand to fully support the contribution of herbs in its development in prehistoric times.

Pictures from the crocus collection, wonderful landscapes in frescoes from the Minoan period (2nd century B.C.) and pots with plant decoration show the importance of herbs in the lives of those people.

and within the large jars was solidified and so the jars remained sealed for nearly 3500 years. On opening these pots, the archaeologists found the remains of herbs and cloth, all charred by the fire but preserved well enough to be identified. The storehouse of this royal building was full of these large pots and, according to first estimates, they were full of products ready for export!

❧ Herbs in tablets

There is a greater amount of evidence proving the liberal use of herbs in the Minoan period (1600-1050 B.C.). There are written accounts (starting from about 1450 B.C.) which help us to identify with certainty the herbs which were recorded on the account tablets of the palace. It can also be appreciated that herbs had a significant role in industry. They were mainly used for aromatic and colouration processes. But there is also no doubt that they were used for medicinal purposes and possibly also in cooking.

In the royal society of the Mycenaean world, the palace buildings were a centre of power as well as of economics. Products for export or domestic use were gathered and stored there. It was in these buildings that the products were processed. Among the herbs which are mentioned in the tablets is coriander.

It is believed that this herb was cultivated in large areas on Crete. At Knossos, the annual crop was 10.000 litres which meant over 220 million seeds!

Apart from coriander, the tablets show cumin, sesame, celery, fennel, crocus, mint, spearmint, rock saphire, Cyperus rotundus and other herbs.

Aeneus' treatment in a Roman mural (Pompei). Virgilius records that Aphrodite brought Cretan dittany to heal his wound.

❧ In ancient Medicine both food and drug

From long ago up until the present day, there have always been those wise voices which strongly recommend the combination of food with medicine. It was Hippocrates, the father of Medicine, who stated that food could also act as a medicine.

It is well known that man looked to nature in ancient times to find medicine. The herbs were used in therapeutic practices, whether as a medicine in themselves or as a carrier of

Ideograms for crocus in Linear A and B script of Crete (2nd millennium B.C.).

an immortal blessing. The gods in the ancient world had an undeniably strong connection with plants and trees, almost being one and the same. Laurel was Apollo's sacred tree. Lettuce was ascribed to Adonis, the poplar tree to Zeus and the olive tree to Athena.

Our enhanced knowledge of herbs in classical Greece helps us to understand the role they played both as medicines and as foods. Doctors in ancient times often refer to the different ways of consuming plants.

It is also important to mention the use of plants in war. Wounds of warriors were treated with herbs! In the legendary story of Aeneus, written by Virgilius in Roman times, we are informed that nature provided a storehouse of treatments to be used in healing injuries. It is said that the goddess Aphrodite raced to Crete to cut a sprig of dittany in order to heal the wounded Aeneus, which legend has it was her son!

➣ Hippocrates' diet

If people lived correctly and ate well then there would be no medicine as there simply would not be any illnesses! It was Hippocrates, the father of Medicine, who expounded this theory thousands of years ago. How many times have modern scientists rushed to use his ideas? This enlightened doctor of the ancient world, who left us with six breakthrough dissertations on diet, assigned an important role to aromatic plants and herbs, believing that food could be enriched with flavours so as to fill someone without having eaten more food. Another greatly enlightened doctor in antiquity, Galenus, split the therapeutic side of Medicine into three areas; diet, surgery and pharmaceutics.

The distinction between food and medicine was very difficult in ancient times. Doctors in anti-quity worked along the line of thought represented by Hippocrates, in that they wanted food to also be a medicine, and so strongly underlined the vital role of good health. These premises set forward by the father of Medicine have not only continued for centuries but have also given the opportunity to other great subsequent doctors to further their research. Food is either hot or cold, so producing either heat or cold.

Galenus (2nd century B.C.), a famous doctor in ancient times, refers in detail to the herbs which can become both food and medicine:

"They are not only food but also medicine. Lettuce is food and also a cold medicine while rocket is both a source of nutrition and a hot medicine. Similarly, mustard, pepper, dill, rue, oregano, mint, savory and thyme are all food stuffs and aromatics which provide heat."

(Galenus, De temperamentis 1,681)

➣ Herbs which slim according to the observations of people in ancient times

Doctors in antiquity placed food stuffs into dietary categories depending on the influence they had on man's life.

The herbs which were recorded in food groupings that helped in slimming are the following, according to Galenus (2nd century B. C.).:

"Garlic, onion, cress, leeks and mustard are those which slim. Someone who does not know about these could make a serious mistake as they are very strong.

At the same time, "smyrnion",

ΘΥΜΕΛΑΙΑ

Harvesting herbs in an icon by Takis Moschos inspired from Byzantine manuscripts (the authors' collection).

"pyrethron", oregano, mint, spearmint, wild mint, savory and thyme all are consumed fresh, before they dry, as when they have dried out, they are medicines and no longer food stuffs." (Galenus, De victu attenuante, 7,1)

In the subsequent years

The ideas of Greek doctors and herbalists influenced Medicine for many centuries as they also affected nutritional advice given. Dioscurides, who refers to 1000 cures which are based on plants, is a continuous source of information, while new experiences and further knowledge is accumulated. In the Byzantine period there were many articles in circulation which mentioned medicinal, nutritional and agricultural advice. "Geoponika" is an example of articles scribed by some of the oldest writers, which were collected by Kassianus Vassus during the reign of the Emperor Constantine Porphyrogenitus (10th century). Subsequent writers seem to have been influenced by this set of articles, such as the Cretan monk Agapius Landus, who lived on Crete and on Mount Athos (17th century). Meanwhile, Medicine in the West is based on the ancient knowledge

Harvesting herbs in an icon by Takis Moschos inspired from Byzantine manuscripts (the authors' collection).

but with the inclusion of more recent observations and studies. At the same time, magic continues to play a part and uses medicinal herbs according to its own methods.

⌁ Medicinal and magical herbs. The "doctors" of Vikos gorge

All over the world there were areas which developed the collection of herbs for therapeutical purposes. Such regions in Greece were the mountains of Pindus, Mount Athos, Taygetus and Crete.

The collection required great care, secrecy and magical processes so as to ensure good results. Herbs were not gathered every day. They were picked on a Thursday or Friday, usually as the sun rose, although it could also be done at midday or midnight, depending on local customs! These magical plants were gathered with a golden tool or they were tied to the tail of a dog so that it could pull the plant out of the ground, thus not endangering the person who was collecting them.

In other places, children collected them or

The Holy Mountain (Athos). A place in Greece that is very well known for its botanic tradition.

TWO HERBS ...

A Greek stamp from 1973 inspired from the Minoan frescoes.

they were blessed at the church. So the scientific side of medicine was tinged with religious rituals or even magical procedures. The therapeutic value of these herbs covered a vast range whether they were protection against "the evil eye", a stimulus for fertility or a treatment for illnesses!

The herb gatherers in Epirus who collected herbs from the gorge of Vikos were well known. For this reason they were named the "Vikojatri", the doctors of Vikos. Moreover in monasteries, formulas from ancient articles were saved and were added to over the years as more knowledge was gained. There are still such articles to be found in Greek monasteries today.

Up until the 20th century, folk medicine was mainly influenced by the knowledge handed down from antiquity and the Byzantine period.

✑ Silphion

Silfion was well known during the Greek and Roman periods and was imported from Northern Africa. Even though it looked like fennel, it did not grow, according to ancient sources, anywhere else apart from the Cyrenaean peninsula, where it was gathered by locals and then exported to various regions.

It was usually combined with vinegar and cheese to flavour dishes which consisted of fish, meat or poultry. This plant, after having been used to flavour the dishes of the Greeks and the Romans, disappeared!

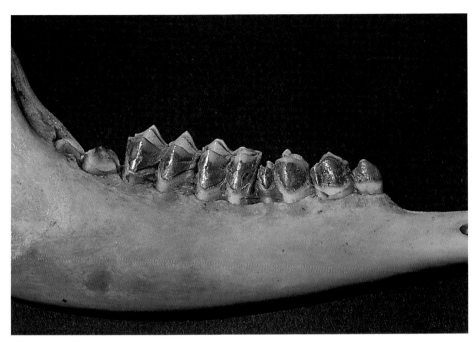

Golden teeth from a sheep in Crete (Karavalakis' collection). It is believed that the plant Polygonum idaeum is the cause of this amazing phenomenon!

∽ The golden herb of Crete

There is a herb which grows on the mountain Psiloritis and it makes the teeth of sheep golden! Neuris (*Polygonum idaeum*) has impressed both shepherds and researchers as in the old days, a magical potion was made from a cutting of this plant and used as a medicine to relieve toothache or open wounds. It was never used in cooking.

Below: Polygonum idaeum in bloom. It is the herb that gives the golden colour to the sheep's teeth.

Saint Anastasia with the herbs and the herb bottle in her hands. An icon by Takis Moschos belonging to the authors.

✑ The saint of herbs!

The saint of herbs is often represented in icons in Byzantine art, holding bottles of medicine and herbs. She is known as Anastasia and she lived during the reign of the Emperor Diocletianus. The Orthodox Church honours her on 22nd December, shortly before Christmas. She was known as "pharmakolytra", the one who saved people with medicine. According to the Synaxarists, Anastasia rushed to the prison where the tortured Christians were being held and treated their wounds with herbs and medicines. In Greece, she is thought of as a doctor-saint! In some areas of Northern Greece, it is customary to make special breads with herbs on her name day. In other regions, people place herbs on her icon!

LET'S CULTIVATE OUR OWN
herb garden

⌐ The creation of a small garden with aromatic and medicinal plants

Specialist shops today sell many herbs and aromatic plants. The rarest are no longer available but some are still used only when fresh (water cress), otherwise they lose a great part of their aroma when dried out (for example, spearmint). That is why it is always a good idea to set aside a corner where a small selection of aromatic and therapeutic plants can be cultivated.

One or more areas should be chosen for the creation of such a garden, all depending on the requirements of the plants which are to be grown. Plants should be put into groups according to their light and soil needs. Most Mediterranean herbs grow in dry areas so a similar place should be chosen. If certain plants require shade, then it is advisable for them to be planted under deciduous trees so that they can get the necessary shade in the summer and sunshine in the winter. If a more moist soil is needed, as in the case of mint, then the ground can be watered more but only in the area around the plant.

Drainage is the greatest problem to be faced with dense soil and so the following information will explain how to prepare the ground so that the plants can flourish. Such a type of garden, known as a rock garden, should be covered in sunshine and be near the kitchen. If the soil is very dense, it would be better to build a small wall, about 40 cm in height, then add good quality garden soil and fully aged manure.

rock garden, it is a good idea to cultivate plants in large clay urns which are 1-1.2 metres. These urns are made with holes in the sides so that between six and eight plants can be cultivated in these holes and not just those in the opening on the top. The plants should be of similar size and require the

A botanical garden in beautiful clay pots, at the Lychnostatis museum, Hersonissos, Crete.

On the bottom, a 10 cm layer of gravel should be placed, followed by about 40 cm of soil. If desired, a few rocks can be added which should be placed so that only a third of the rock shows and so gives the look of a natural setting.

If you do not want to build a wall, a corner can be taken up whereby a layer of gravel is placed and then on top, the soil and the dung are added. If you want to lessen the density of the garden soil, this can be achieved by mixing it with grains of river sand and dung. A good, balanced mixture is 3:1:1, in other words, three parts soil, one part dung or turf and one part sand.

If there is no room for a

same amount of moisture so that there are no problems with any rivalry.

Plants for the rock garden can be found at garden centres or can be cultivated. These plants are produced from seeds, rhizomes, bulbs, nodules, shoots and grafts. The sowing time of native Mediterranean plants is in the autumn.

Planting can be done at any time of the year but should be avoided in the spring and summer due to the high temperatures which then necessitate excessive watering that rots the roots. Furthermore, some plants grow new shoots very quickly and, due to their vulnerability, they cannot tolerate the heat and long exposure to the sun.

Watering of the garden

If the garden is built at the end of autumn or the beginning of winter, watering can be done by sprinklers and one or two times is enough, as the weather is usually quite wet during this season. If the planting is done in the spring or summer, watering should be in drops and there should not be a great deal of moisture in the soil as this can cause diseases.

Watering during the summer months should be carried out at long intervals, so as to merely maintain the garden and not to encourage the development of the plants. As in their natural surroundings, these plants grow during the winter months and in spring, because these are the most suitable seasons for them.

Annual, biennial and perennial

Herbs can be annual, biennial or perennial. The annual herbs, such as rocket, basil, chervil, dill, borage and mustard, complete their cycle of life after one year and are propagated by seeds.

The biennials, like parsley, live for two years, but you can always have them in your garden as long as you sow them two successive years. In the first year these plants grow and in the second year they produce seeds which fall to the ground and re-grow. The perennial plants, for example, lemon verbena, savory, thyme, mint and rosemary, live for more than two years and complete their reproductive cycle every year.

The seeds of the biennials and the perennials need three weeks to take seed so it is better to get them from a nursery.

Among the roses in Diakophto, Peloponnese, an area with rich botanic tradition.

⇜ Harvesting

The harvesting of herbs is carried out when the plant is at a suitable biological stage so that its essential oils are at their peak. This particular stage may vary from one plant to another.

Usually, the leaves and green parts of the plant are collected at the point when the plant is in full growth, just before blooming, while the flowered parts of the plant are harvested at the beginning of blooming, so that they keep the most smell and the bees can take as much nectar as possible

The plants should not be uprooted, but the shoots should be cut with a sharp tool. If so desired, fruits and seeds can be collected but these should be fully ripe. Roots, bulbs and in general underground shoots should be gathered in autumn and winter when the vegetative cycle of the plant has been completed.

Cretan cistus.

Picking greens and herbs in Elympos, on the island of Karpathos.

ATTENTION!

☞ *Gathering should be done in the morning and after the first moisture has dried out from the plants.*
Collecting herbs and green plants should be avoided from areas which are not clean, fields sprayed with insecticides and the sides of roads, so as to lessen the possibilty of poisoning, exhaust fumes and animal excretion.

Harvesting rosemary on Crete.

☙ Drying out

Drying should be done in a shady place. In this way the natural colour and chemical structure of the plant can be retained. The drying out process is of great importance for plants with essential oils, even if this does take a long time.

To establish that the plant has fully dried out, a bunch of dried shoots should be squeezed. If the leaves shatter and the shoots do not bend but instead break, then they are totally dried out. It is best to place the herbs on paper or netting so that they are best ventilated and thus dry out quicker. They should be turned over from time to time to aid the drying process. If there is only a small amount, the shoots can be tied together in small, loose bunches and hung from the ceiling of an outhouse or storeroom or a place where they will be aired well. The better the ventilation, the quicker they will dry out. The look and smell of the herbs are maintained after the drying out process, but they are slightly less in weight. This is the reason why in cooking a smaller amount of dried herbs are used than if they were fresh (about a third of the amount of a fresh herb). However it is not worth drying out all herbs. Herbs such as parsley, rocket, dill or cilantro are available all year round. Also worth mentioning is the fact that green herbs, with the exception of lemon verbena, mint and tarragon, do not retain their aroma after having been dried out. The woody herbs like savory, thyme, sage, Cretan dittany, "adonajida", oregano, lavender and marjoram not only dry out easily but retain very nearly the exact same strong smell.

An oregano picker on the island of Naxos.

☞ **Take care**: A microwave cannot be used in the process of drying out as it destroys flavour and could start a fire.

☞ **Storage:** Preferably, dried herbs should be stored in a glass jar or clay pot in a dark place where there is no moisture. At first, the jars should not be closed tightly as there could still be some moisture inside, so it is a good idea to place some rice in a piece of gauze and put this in the container so that it can absorb any remaining moisture. Never forget to put a label on the outside of each jar noting which herb is inside and the date of gathering, because dried herbs should be used within one to one and half years.

Above: Drying herbs in Greek houses.

Left: A young herb picker from the island of Corfu.
Postcard, beginning of 20th century (the authors' collection).

OTHER FORMS OF PRESERVATION

Freezing: Herbs which cannot be dried out can be kept in the freezer as long as they have been blanched a little. If you wish to keep a small amount of leaves, you can put them in a jar and place the jar in the freezer. Another method is to finely chop the herbs and store them in ice cube trays in the freezer.

Pesto sauce: Apart from being used with spaghetti, meat and fish, pesto sauce is another way of preserving herbs. This sauce contains a certain herb or combination of herbs, along with olive oil which greatly helps in the process of preservation. (For further information, look at the pages concerning the recipes).

PERFUMES, HERBS AND PLAGUE: Physicians in 18th century believed that they were protected against plague, the terrible infectious disease that killed millions of people, with the use of perfumes and herbs. When they visited their patients, they hid their bodies inside leather clothes and adjusted a beaky nose on their face inside which they put perfumes. Perfumes, however, were made from herbs. In even earlier times, a man accompanied the physician and burnt aromatic plants inside the patient's room. In this way they believed that the air "was filtered" and they could not get infected!

HERBS AND
health

"Don't worry, my love, the world is not lost,
with the herbs of the earth, all illnesses will be cured"

A Cretan couplet

The history of Medicine has shown that herbs have had the leading role! Observations and centuries of experience have often provided impressive solutions to health problems which people have suffered. Even in ancient times, it was seen that some certain herbs had tonic-like qualities, others helped someone to relax and others were an antiseptic, painkillers or stomachache reliefs. Today, in various laboratories around the world, hundreds of plants are examined and tested in the search for new medicines. As a basic rule of Medicine, prevention is always preferred over treatment. Therefore, the recommendations of all international organisations turn towards the idea that modern man takes on balanced dietary habits. Fruit and vegetables are the types of food which should be on our tables at mealtimes every day.

Herbs are rich sources of antioxidants, substances which protect the human organism from cardiovascular diseases and various forms of cancer but to name just a few. There has recently been a great deal of discussion about fatty acids ω3, which are found in herbs, green vegetables, nuts and fatty fish and ultimately provide a shield of protection for our health. Unfortunately, today's western type diet is poor in such fatty acids, yet rich in ω6 acids, which can be found in seed oil, eggs and meat from

farmed animals.

The enormous effect of herbs on the digestive system through the use of herbs in cooking is of vital importance.

Fresh herbs and vegetables are rich in essential oils, yet it should not be overlooked that even the preserved or dried products of these food groups still retain a high percentage.

BE WARNED!

*T*his book does not recommend medicines or potions. It looks at herbs, just like greens or vegetables, as an extremely valuable aid which helps modern man to fully enjoy traditional cooking, something which has been practised for hundreds of years and provides a much healthier style of eating and therefore life!

☞ It should be noted, however, that herbs are looked upon as medicines, in that they are used for therapeutic purposes. Many medicines can be harmful, when used in large or prolonged dosages. Dosages should be carefully controlled, as with any medicine. Before using any herb on a daily basis for a long period of time, ensure that you have been fully informed so as to avoid any bad side effects. If you wish to use a herb for therapeutic purposes, consult your doctor.

If you do not recognise a herb or green, it is always better not to use it. Common names vary and often the same name can refer to a range of plants! It is only the scientific name which can ensure the identity of each plant. The plants which are mentioned here are also referred to with their scientific name.

HERBS IN
diet

Let's return to the richest diet in taste and health! Herbs, greens and vegetables can help us in this! At this point, we should acknowledge the difference between herbs and greens although this can be quite difficult, as most plants at some time or another have been used for therapeutic purposes. Quite simply, we could continue with the belief that doctors had in ancient times: that they are used both as food and medicine.

Of course, this all depends on the way that they are used. However, here it should be stated that when they are used as a food, they do not lose (or at least, not entirely lose) the substances which are believed to be of so much value to our health.

The region which consumes the most greens is, without doubt, the Mediterranean. On Crete, the consumption of greens is a way of life.

It is well worth noting that most of these are eaten in their raw state. Not only are they delicious uncooked but provide the opportunity for a variety of combinations, such as the famous traditional Greek salad or the "owl", a dried rusk with finely chopped tomatoes on top, garnished with some feta cheese and oregano. It is no coincidence that the Cretan diet is thought to be the healthiest in the world!

An abundance of cultivated and wild greens are used on Crete, but the aromatic herbs are used in moderation, as the islanders prefer a more authentic taste. In the Peloponnese, herbs are used to enrichen tastes further. Even the strong smelling oregano from Taygetus is used as a vegetable in its own right!

Every country has its own particular customs with flavour and we can often see a country identify itself with one particular herb. If oregano is a favourite all over the Mediterranean, then dill and parsley are the herbs which are most used in Greece, thyme in southern Italy and southern France, coriander in Cyprus and in the countries in northern Africa.

Herbs with olive oil

The cooking of vegetables, greens and herbs must be seen as a return of modern man to a healthier diet.

Dishes with vegetables, a tradition which supported the farmers on Crete, the Cyclades, the Dodecanese, the Peloponnese and the southern regions of Italy for centuries, all use olive oil.

The full flavour of this heavenly product not only combines ideally with the finished dish, using greens and herbs, but also proves to be a true treasure for good health.

The recipes which have been chosen for this book mainly use olive oil.

It is an ecological perception on life which can lead anyone to healthier dietary habits but also to unbelievable gastronomic pleasures.

A book about olive oil

Further information about olive oil, the civilisation it dominated, its production, special points, the way in which it is used, along with 150 recipes to be tried out and fully enjoyed in your own home, can be found in "The secret of good health: Olive oil".

Green food every day!

Scientific research in the last few decades has strongly urged the adoption of a daily diet like the farmers in the poor areas in the Mediterranean, especially on Crete.

These people feed off the land and so attain the full nutritional value that is offered. It goes without saying that vegetables and fruit are to be found on their tables at meal times, along with grain and olive oil. Red meat is rarely seen, maybe once a week, although in the old days, it was eaten only a few times each year.

Fish, cheese and white meat, as in chicken, are seen more often in their diet, perhaps even twice a week.

TASTY DISHES WITH
herbs

E ven the simplest dish, a common every day meal, can be made very attractive and can take on a different flavour and aroma, just by using a herb. In general, it is best to know which herbs are most suited to certain food groups. A grilled pork chop can gain added flavour with a little thyme or oregano. Just the smell of a herb can change our appetite!

Herbs are generally used in small amounts in order to add flavour and aroma to a dish, to bring out the best in it. Sometimes, though, they can be used to such an extent that they become the main ingredient of the dish! On Crete, chicken can be cooked with parsley but the herb is added in such large amounts that it is looked upon more as a vegetable. Such wonderful dishes are often seen on tables at mealtimes throughout the Mediterranean.

ᴖ Herbs and their use in creative cooking

In the markets of ancient Athens (the city where the most information was saved), there was an abundance of herbs which of course were used in the diet of the Athenians. Among the readily available herbs were celery, fennel, chickory, lettuce, nettle, cress and the tender peaks of palm trees.

The use of aromatic herbs strongly indicates that in ancient times in Greece, there were the first forms of creative cooking in Europe.

Special aromatic bread with dill or poppy seeds, sweets and dishes, all give a clear picture of the first uses of herbs in cooking.

It could be said that this style of cooking perfectly combines the desire for a better taste and the attitude of doctors concerning healthy food.

During the time of the Roman Empire, gastronomic developments continued and even the Romans in the provinces managed to use herbs in their diet. The logic behind all this was what had been supported by doctors since ancient times: herbs are both a source of food and medicine!

ᴖ The ancient "myma". Herb cooking

A dish has been passed down to us by Epaenetus, a writer in the first century B.C. It is "myma". This dish constitutes evidence of the very ancient use of small cut pieces of meat (like minced meat) but cooked with a variety of herbs. It is a sweet and sour dish that was cooked by famous chefs in the ancient world. Not only was it made with meat, but also with fish, using nine different kinds of herbs and spices (thirteen seasonings in all):

"It is made with every meat from sacrifice and also with poultry. The soft meat is finely chopped, along with the spleen and the intestines.

This meat and the blood are mixed with vinegar, grilled cheese, silfion, cumin, fresh and dried thyme, savory, fresh and dried coriander, "gition" (*this plant has not been recognised*), browned onion or poppies, raisins or honey and sour pomegranate seeds. You can make "myma" with fish as well" (Athenaeus 662,e-f).

Not long after, the Romans started to use other spices and herbs, such as chamomile and cardamom, sage and the aromatic cyperus which had been used in the Mycenaean times in order to add an aroma to oil.

GETTING ACQUAINTED WITH
THE COMMONEST

herbs

Dill (Anethum graveolens)
Family: Umbelliferae

- **HARVESTING:** The foliage can be harvested at any time, the seeds when ripe.
- **DESCRIPTION:** An annual, cultivated herb with a heavy scent which came originally from S. E. Asia and India. It is 20-80 cm tall with tripinnatisect leaves and delicately laciniate leaflets which clasp the smooth grooved sea green stem. The flowers are yellow and bear dense umbels with 15-30 unequal rays. The fruit is ovoid – elliptic.
- **MEDICINE:** The leaves and especially the seeds contain essential oil rich in limonene and carvone and for this reason it was used as an emollient and a tonic for the muscles of athletes. As a medicine, it was given to infants for colic and other gastrointestinal disorders. It is also a galactagogue, stimulant and diuretic.
- **FLAVOURING WINE:** In ancient Greece, dill was added to flavour wine. According to Dioscurides, it was used in the preparation of the "anethinon myron" and the "anethinon wine". According to Byzantine Kassianus Vassus, wine was made with dill seeds (wrapped in a delicate cloth and left within the wine during the

fermentation), which was able to cure dysuria. It was also used as sleep inducer.

• **USAGE:** Dill was known and, in all probability, used on Crete and the Aegean islands 4000 years ago, although we don't know how. As Alexis states, dill was used for flavouring a famous dish of the ancient world, which was named "kandavlos" and prepared with boiled meat, bread crumbs, cheese and dill.

Today it is utilized both in cooking and in bread making (the green parts as well as the seeds), especially the seeds, which can flavour drinks. Dill can be used as an ingredient for pickles, meat, fish (especially salmon), French choucroute, salads, soups, sauces, stuffed vegetables, meatballs, cheese, omelets, vegetables and pulses. It is one of the herbs used for flavouring olive oil and vinegar. Dill is a very good match with cucumber, consequently it can be used in every dish containing cucumber, like the well known Greek tzatziki. Likewise, it goes very well with dishes in an egg-lemon sauce. In such dishes it can be one of the main ingredients, for example when cooking meat with dill in egg-lemon sauce, dill is used as a vegetable, in large amount.

"Adonajida" (Origanum microphyllum)
Family: Labiatae

• **HARVESTING:** June - July.

• **DESCRIPTION:** A short aromatic shrub, 20-50 cm tall or more if it is cultivated. It has many thin quadrangular shoots growing from the base. It is a hairy herb, with ovate or cordate leaves of white-green colour. The flowers are purple-pink, 5 mm long and grow in terminal racemose inflorescences, blooming from June to September depending on the altitude. It grows wild in dry rocky areas, 300-800 m high. It is indigenous to Crete, nevertheless, it is not widely known, as it grows in few specific areas close to Dicte Mountain and the White Mountains on Crete. It is the herb of the future!

In certain areas on Crete (villages of the province of Malevizi and elsewhere) another herb with whitish dentate leaves and creamy-yellow flowers is known by the name "adonajida". It is a member of the same family and is named **Teucrium capitatum**.

Note: A natural hybrid of Origanum microphyllum and Origanum vulgare has been traced to the area of Lassithi on Crete. The new plant seems to combine the characteristics of the parent plants and probably has important therapeutic qualities. It needs further research.

• **ADONIS' HERB.** "Adonajida" has been said to be the herb of Adonis, the most handsome man of antiquity, who Aphrodite, the goddess of beauty, fell in love with! According to a more recent Cretan myth, Adonajida was once a beautiful girl who wandered in the mountains and gathered flowers and aromatic plants. One day she was attacked by a wild pig and was killed! However, the god, Adonis, felt pity for her and transformed her into a shrub, to grow eternally in the mountains and smell like the herbs that she had gathered when she hab been alive.

The ancient myth has some things in common with the modern one: Adonis is killed by a wild goat, just as Adonajida is! In the end they are both transformed into flowers...

• **THE RESUSCITATING HERB.** It is said on Crete that if somebody wants to learn to play the lyre beautifully, he must go and play it at a crossroad at midnight. The Nereids will soon gather around him and will teach him the secrets of music. However, he has to be within a circle which he has marked with his dagger and in no way should he step out of it.

Once upon a time a shepherd took his lyre every night and went to the crossroad to play it. A Nereid, the most beautiful of all, fell in love with him. One night, unfortunately, the shepherd forgot to mark the circle! The Nereids gathered there, except the one who was in love with him. She was away... The young man started playing the lyre but the Nereids didn't like the melody and began to drag and hit him until, a short time before dawn, they killed him! At that moment his Nereid arrived. On seeing him, she started crying. She didn't know what to do as only a few minutes were left till the dawn when she had to disappear from earth. A humble herb emitted a wonderful odour close to her. It was "adonajida"! She cut a few sprigs, brushed them on the face and chest of her beloved shepherd and his heart started beating again. He had been resuscitated! Without the Nereid realizing it, the day had broken... She should have left before dawn, but she hadn't! She left together with the young man and they lived happily ever after. The herb had given life to the shepherd and had made the Nereid a mortal woman.

• **MEDICINE:** Popular medicine suggests "adonajida" tea for a sore throat, cold, diarrhoea etc. It contains 0,44-1,68% of essential oil (weight of dried flowered herbs).

• **USAGE:** "Adonajida" makes a very tasty and aromatic infusion. Due to its very sweet scent, it can be mixed with other herbs which are not so tasty.

Scented-leaved pelargonium
(Pelargonium odoratissimum)
Family: Geraniaceae

- **HARVESTING:** All year round.
- **DESCRIPTION:** A perennial herbaceous plant, 0.5-1 m tall, in the shape of a hemi-spherical shrub, originated from S. Africa. It has downy, wrinkled, ovate, deeply dissected, lobed, sweet-smelling leaves. The inflorescences are lilac, growing from the edges of the plant. It is a hardy plant growing on any soil.
- **MEDICINE:** Popular medicine suggests the use of scented-leaved pelargonium infusion for digestive problems, and its juice for skin diseases. It is also considered to be a calmative and a sedative.
- **USAGE:** In addition to its use as an infusion, by itself or in combination with other herbs, it serves to flavour sweets with fruit, notably spoon sweets (cherry, sour cherry, grapes and quince, to which scented-leaved pelargonium is an excellent match).

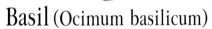

Basil (Ocimum basilicum)
Family: Labiatae

- **HARVESTING:** Preferably in the summer, when the inflorescences appear.
- **DESCRIPTION:** It comes originally from the tropical areas. It belongs to the Ocimum genus which comprises 60 members. There are species with large leaves, almost 10 cm in dimension, which are used on Crete to wrap the stuffing for "dolmathes", a very delicious dish! The scent of each species differs, it can remind of lemon, incense, cinnamon, clove etc. The name is derived from the Greek word *basileus*, king.

An annual or perennial (in warm climates) herbaceous plant, 20-100 cm tall, with ovate, entire or dentate, green, violet or blackish leaves and small flowers, white or pinkish, arranged in terminal spikes.

It is a wide-ranging species regarding the size and colour of the leaves etc., bearing different names, such as *curly, broad-leaved, "athanatos" (immortal)* and others. A common aromatic plant, it requires soil rich in organic substances, that is manure (the secret of success). It needs a fair amount of water and if it remains thirsty for a while, it blooms and dies soon.

- **MEDICINE:** Hippocrates regarded basil as beneficial for the heart and prescribed it for the treatment of constipation and as an antiemetic (against vomiting). Pliny suggested vinegar scented with basil against fainting.

Dioscurides (2, 141) considered it to be soothing for the abdomen, a diuretic and a galactagogue. He prescribed its juice for the treatment of the clouding of the eyes and catarrh. He also mentions (1, 67) that basil was the basic ingredient of a cologne, the "okiminon myron". Popular medicine attributes it with spasmolytic, calmative and eupeptic properties.

• FROM ALEXANDER THE GREAT TO SAINT ELENI

It is believed that it was Alexander the Great who propagated basil in the Mediterranean. He saw it in India, was very impressed and his army brought it to Europe. Nevertheless, it is certain that the Greeks knew basil long before Alexander's campaign, and it is mentioned by poets who lived before him.

Greek popular tradition connects this plant with Aghia Eleni: When she went to Palestine looking for Christ's cross, she saw a sweet-smelling shrub. She thought it to be a sign from God. She dug under its root and found the cross, the most sacred symbol of Christianity!

• **USAGE:** It has numerous culinary uses, as a flavouring agent and to enrich the taste of many dishes. It is a good match with tomato and can be used wherever tomatoes are used, but it also goes well with other vegetables, soups, salads, eggs, seafood, meat and game. It is used to add flavour to meatballs, stuffing for vegetables, bread, cakes, biscuits, fruit juice, sweet preserves etc.

The well known Italian pesto has basil as its main ingredient (see the recipe in the chapter concerning sauces). It should be used fresh, as dried basil has lost most of its flavour. When used in cooked dishes it should be added towards the end for better and stronger flavour.

• **AROMATIC "KYKEON":** Hippocrates makes mention of a drink or creamy preparation which initially had a ritualistic character -see more in the chapter: mint). That dish was named "kykeon" and was flavoured with basil, mint, celery root, coriander, dill and poppy.

Anise (Pimpinella anisum)
Family: Umbelliferae

• **HARVESTING:** The green parts are harvested before it blooms, in July – August, and the seeds later, after they have matured and turned brown but before they fall off the head.

• **DESCRIPTION:** An annual cultivated plant, originally from Asia and N. Africa, with an erect stem, 50-80 cm tall. It has simple basal leaves with ovate dentate leaflets, while the stem leaves have linear leaflets. The flowers are white or yellowish, arranged in loose umbels, 6-12 rayed. The fruits are ovoid or oblong, 3-5 mm long, hairy and strongly fragrant.

There are 4 varieties, the best being the Spanish, due to its strong flavour. Anise is no relation to star-anise (*Illicum verum*), which is a shrub cultivated in Japan and China and contains essential oils with approximately the same consistency.

- **HISTORY:** Anise was known in ancient times and the Egyptians used it, together with cumin and marjoram, for the mummification of the dead.

Even in those ancient years it was used for medicinal purposes and magic practices. It was also used as a flavouring agent in various sweets and breads.

- **MEDICINE:** The aniseeds contain essential oil composed mainly of anethol. Today the essential oil of the anise is considered to be a diuretic, digestive, expectorant, spasmolytic, galactagogue, tonic and strong carminative. It should be taken in moderate doses.

The ancient Greeks and Romans regarded anise as an aphrodisiac (it induces sexual desire, according to Dioscurides -3,56) and believed that it keeps people young and averts bad dreams when placed under the pillow at night. They also believed that travellers on long journeys should take anise drinks in order to have a pleasant time.

Hippocrates believed that anise stops sneezing and used it against the bad smell of the genitals. Dioscurides recommended it as a diuretic and sudatory and for headaches. Pliny states that if women going into labour smelled anise, they had an easy delivery.

- **"ANISITIS WINE":** Anise seeds were used in the making of wine during the Byzantine times. They believed that it was good for "dysuria and the interior organs" (Kassianus Vassus 8,4).

- **USAGE:** Not only the green parts but also the flowers and seeds, either whole or ground, are used to flavour eggs, cheese, fruit, meat, fish, salads, bread, cookies, biscuits and alcoholic drinks. The characteristic aniseed taste occurs in various Mediterranean drinks (Greek ouzo, Spanish anisette, French pastis). It is one of the ingredients of Curry, the well known herb and spice mixture, together with curcuma or saffron, cardamom, ginger, coriander, pepper and other seasonings.

- **THE ANISE-FLAVOURED APPLES OF A 17TH CENTURY MONK**
  In 17th century the Cretan monk Agapius Landus, who wrote one book with agricultural and dietary recommendations, advised his readers to eat apples cooked with sugared anise. He believed that apples were more wholesome that way!

Purslane (Portulaca oleracea)
Family: Portulacaceae

• **HARVESTING:** June – July.

• **DESCRIPTION:** This is an annual hairless, succulent plant with many stems, creeping or slightly erect. The leaves are obovate – oblong with a cuneate base. The flowers are yellow, stalkless, at the axils or at the tops of the stems, solitary or in clusters. The seeds are black inside an ovoid capsule. There are varieties with larger leaves and stems. It is indigenous to the Mediterranean and grows on arable land, especially in wet gardens.

• **MEDICINE:** Hippocrates regarded purslane as a treatment for female disorders and specifically for the haemorrhaging of the uterus, Galenus for tooth and gum benumbing and Dioscurides for eye conditions. The latter, too (2,124), believes that it helps the wounds heal and that it is a medicine for the stomach and haemorrhoids. Popular medicine used it against fever, a practice having its roots in ancient Greece!
Medicine has lately conducted a lot of research on this herb and the results are astonishing: The biological value of purslane is great because, apart from the various vitamins, it contains the famous ω3 acid which lowers the cholesterol level in the blood.

• **USAGE:** It has a sourish taste and is mostly used raw in salads, but it can be cooked as well in soups or with fish or meat, as a vegetable. It can also be pickled and preserved for winter salads. The 16th–17th travellers who visited Egypt describe a refreshing preparation that was given to patients with fever: purslane with yogurt! Even today, a special salad is prepared with purslane and yoghurt. It is one of the commonest salads in Crete during the summer months.

• **THE MONK'S RECIPE:** Agapius Landus, that erudite monk of 17th century, regarded purslane as a "cold" herb and suggested that it should be eaten with basil, rocket, cress, garlic etc. According to Magda Ohnefalsch Richter, purslane was an excellent ingredient for soups in Cyprus in 19th century.

Apollo and Daphne on coins of 3rd c. B.C.
Left and right: the god wearing a laurel wreath on his head (Amphipolis,
Macedonia and Olynthus). Center: Apollo holding a laurel branch (a coin of the Delphic amphictyony).

Bay laurel (Laurus nobilis)
Family: Lauraceae

• **HARVESTING:** Any time of the year, yet it is better for the leaves to be harvested towards the end of summer.

• **DESCRIPTION:** The laurel is an evergreen tree, also found in the form of a shrub, indigenous to the Mediterranean. The leaves are leathery, dark green and lance-shaped. The flowers are borne at the leaf axils, in groups of 4-6 and are strongly fragrant. The fruit is an ovoid black berry, similar in size to the fruit of the wild olive tree.

Caution: Bay laurel should not be mistaken for cherry laurel (prunus laurocerasus) which is also grown in England. The leaves of cherry laurel are poisonous and should not be consumed.

• **MEDICINE:** Medicinal properties have been attributed to laurel since prehistoric times. Hippocrates administered it as an analgesic after delivery and for female disorders. He also cured sterility with it. Dioscurides (1st century) recommended its decoction for ailments of the bladder and the uterus, its mashed fruits against asthma and tuberculosis and their juice in cases of hard hearing and fatigue (I,78). In popular medicine it is considered to be eupeptic, antirheumatic and against arthritis deformans. It is also used in hair treatment and dyeing. Laurel oil is extracted by mechanical processing of the fruits and ethereal oil by distillation of the leaves. Oil of excellent quality is produced in the monasteries of Mount Athos by boiling the fruits.

• **LAUREL WINE:** The Byzantines flavoured wine with bay laurel and used it as diuretic, against coughing and neurological disorders ("it is good for hysterical women").

- **HISTORY:** It has been cultivated since Homeric times (Odyssey I, 83). It was a sacred tree in ancient years, the tree of ceremonies and wreaths. At Delphi, Pythia, Apollo's priestess who foretold people the will of the Gods, chewed bay leaves! At Thebes, the most handsome young men participated in the holy ceremonies, holding laurel branches.

Balls hang from the ends of the branches, which symbolized the sun, the moon and the stars. Who said that ancient people didn't know the shape of the celestial bodies?

The Romans crowned the winners at the games with laurel garlands. From this custom, the academic terms Baccalaureat, Bachelor, Bach, lier, which are awarded to university graduates, are derived. For example, Baccalaureat from Bacca (fruit) and Laurus (laurel), which means a laurel branch with fruit.

Apollo and Daphne on a Greek stamp (engraving by A. Tassos, 1958).

- **THE LOVE OF THE HANDSOME GOD:** In Greek mythology Daphne was an extremely beautiful Nymph, the daughter of a river-god, Peneios or Lathonas, and Ge (the Earth), at the time when people personified Ge as the wife of Uranus (the Sky). It is reported that Apollo fell in love with her and started chasing her in the woods. When he got very close to her, the fair Nymph asked her father (or her mother as well) to protect her so as to keep her virginity. So they transformed her into a tree. Daphne is depicted on an ancient mosaic in Cyprus, at the moment when branches are starting to grow from her body! It seems, though, that the god fell in love with the tree as well. He made a wreath with sprigs of the tree and put it around his head. People gave Apollo a second name, after Daphne: They named him Apollo Daphnetes.

As he was the god of purification himself, his priests used laurel as a means of purification. Vranchus, one of Apollo's foretellers, used the laurel sprigs in purification practices and rid the inhabitants of the town of Miletus from the plague.

- **THE SYMBOL OF VICTORY:** Apollo was in search of a place to build his sanctuary and he went to Delphi. There he found Python, a terrible dragon. He managed to kill him and liberated the area. Then he cut sprigs from a laurel tree in a forest that was nearby, made a wreath and was crowned with it. It was the sign that the god had won! Since then, laurel is regarded as the symbol of victory. In the music games during the Pythia, a celebration in honour of Apollo, the winners got a precious prize: they were crowned with a laurel wreath!

- **USAGE:** Dried bay leaves are widely used in the kitchen, either whole or crushed, because they are less bitter than fresh ones. They add an excellent flavour to soups, tomato juice, stews, simmered meats, meat or fish in the oven or on the grill, chickpeas in the oven, lentil soup, creams, fruit salads etc. Olive oil can be perfectly scented with bay leaves and it is widely used in popular medicine. Bay leaves have been used in traditional baking for centuries, in the baking of the wonderful aromatic "eftazymo" (chick pea bread). Don't be surprised if you see the Beduins use bay leaves when making their coffee as the people of the African desert like their coffee prepared in that way. Bay leaves are also placed in the jars with the dried fruit (namely figs and raisins) to ward off various insects.

• **THE "KAMMATA" OF SPARTA:** In ancient Sparta special ritual sweets were made to be offered to the gods. They were called "kammatides" and had the smell of laurel because they were wrapped in bay leaves.

Rosemary (Rosmarinus officinalis)
Family: Labiatae

• **HARVESTING:** Any time of the year but mostly in the summer and autumn.
• **DESCRIPTION:** It is a woody evergreen shrub, indigenous to the Mediterranean. It can grow to a height of 0,5-1 meter or more, if the soil is rich. It has linear, leathery leaves, green above and white below and blue-white flowers borne in spikes at the leaf axils.

• **MEDICINE:** As a pharmaceutical plant, which is also indicated by its name (officinalis), it has important qualities: It is an excellent stimulant, spasmolytic, cholagogic, carminative, strong emmenagogic and abortive. Gargles with rosemary tea soothe mouth ulcers and a sore throat. External use: Rosemary leaves boiled in wine can be applied on sprained and painful joints, on wounds and eczemas, with good results. In ancient times it was used to heal jaundice. Galenus recommended rosemary boiled in wine for stomach and abdominal pains (De remediis parabilibus 14,558).

ATTENTION*: It must be used in moderation because its overuse can cause poisoning, even death!*

• **IT REJOICES THE GODS:** According to the myths of the ancient Greeks, there was once a man who went by the name of Lebanus and was devoted to the gods from a young age. However, impious people killed him. Ge, who honours the gods, transformed him into a plant, to smell and please the gods with its sweet scent! It was often used as incense in antiquity. It is probably Dioscurides' "Fourth Lebanotis", which was called Rosmaninun by the Romans.

- **SUPPLICATION TO THE GODS**: Rosemary was often burnt on altars to the ancient gods. Its scent conveyed people's supplications to the gods. In ancient Egypt, it was the plant which scented not only the world of the living but also that of the dead.

It was put in the tombs of the Pharaohs, to transfer its fragrance into the world of the souls.

- **USAGE**: It adds flavour to meat, sausages, poultry, fish, seafood, cheese sauces, omelets, fruit salads, spinach, soups and peas. In certain Mediterranean cuisines, lamb is often cooked with rosemary.

It imparts its aroma to meat on the grill if you put a few rosemary sprigs in the charcoals.

It marries well with citrus fruits and is used extensively in bread making. It is the necessary ingredient of "savore", a sauce made with olive oil and vinegar. This sauce combines best with potatoes, vegetables, fish, liver and snails, fried in olive oil. It also flavours olive oil, vinegar, wine and can be used as a tea.

Cretan dittany, erontas
(Origanum dictamnus)
Family: Labiatae

- **HARVESTING:** During the flowering period (June – October).
- **DESCRIPTION:** A short shrub with hairy stems branched from the base and reaching a height of 40 cm. The whole plant is hairy and has a downy appearance. The leaves are white-green, round or ovate of the same length and width, 15 (4-30) mm. The flowers are pink, 11(8-15) mm long. It is indigenous to Crete and grows wild in many parts of the island, on unapproachable limestone slopes, at an altitude of 0-1900 m.

The plant has considerable economic interest for Crete. It is the only herb which is cultivated owing to its high price in the market. This fact helped it survive as a wild plant. In former times its price was as high as 1 gold pound per kilo and quite a few people lost their lives in their effort to pick it on steep slopes. Currently 2 varieties are cultivated in the area of Embaros, the narrow-leafed and the broad-leafed. The former has a stronger scent while the latter yields more in its dried condition.

- **MEDICINE:** The herb's content in volatile oil is 1,33-1,6% and its main ingredient is carvacrol (58-82%), which justifies its germicidal action. In the ancient world it was in great demand and was surrounded with holy traditions. A cataplasm for the wounds was made with dittany, which was regarded as sacred, because it was said that they had found it written on a scroll at the sanctuary of Memphis.

The wounded wild goat chews Cretan dittany in order to be cured and get rid of the arrow, as depicted by Dapper (1668).

Hippocrates considered it "okytokion", (facilitating childbirth) and Dioscurides believed that it aborted dead foetuses. Popular medicine uses it to heal interior wounds and to alleviate stomachache and a sore throat.

• **THE HERB THAT SAVED AENEUS.** Aeneus, goddess Aphrodite's son, owed his life to dittany: After the battle of Troy, Aeneus went to Italy where he was connected with the founding of Rome.
During one of the most crucial duels there, he was seriously hurt. According to Virgilius, Aphrodite raced to Crete, cut some dittany and with it, she healed him:
The arrow was expelled from the wound and the pain stopped! Virgilius was inspired by the ancient story which is also recorded by many other writers (e.g. Aristoteles) and according to which, if a wild goat got hurt by a hunter's arrow, it ran to find some dittany, chewed it and the arrow was expelled!

• **HERB OF THE GODDESS OF CHILD-BIRTH.** In ancient times, dittany was the herb of Eleuthia, the goddess who aided pregnant women to give birth!
She was succeeded by Artemis. It is recorded that there was a statue of her crowned with a wreath of dittany.

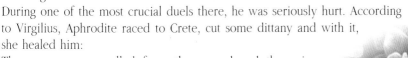

- **HERB OF LOVE.** It was named "Aphrodite's lip" in antiquity.
On Crete, it is the herb of love and is actually known by this name (erontas = love). In Medieval times, if someone wanted to express his love, he climbed mountains or steep rocks, tied himself with ropes, cut a beautiful bunch of dittany and offered it to his beloved.
The herb was considered aphrodisiac in older times.

- **USAGE:** Despite its wide and significant use in the preparation of infusions and drinks (benedictine, drinks by the Italian firm *Martini & Rossi*), it has no application in traditional cooking.
Recently it has started being used in creative cooking and sweet making. On Crete, it served to flavour wine.

Peppermint (Mentha x piperita)
Family: Labiatae

- **HARVESTING:** It is usually harvested prior to flowering but if it is intended for the extraction of its essential oil, it is harvested in full flower (June to August – September).
- **DESCRIPTION:** A number of herbs are known by the name of mint, many of which have nothing in common with the real mint, peppermint. It is an aromatic plant known and appreciated since antiquity. It is derived from the crossing of Mentha aquatica and Mentha spicata (spearmint) and has survived owing to its cultivation. It is propagated by vegetative means, rooted stolons with shoots, because the plant is sterile, it doesn't produce any seeds.
This is a perennial herbaceous plant, with a strong fragrance. It has an erect quadrangular stem which is branched above and can reach a height of 30-90 cm. The cultivated varieties are smooth or slightly hairy plants with lanceolate, dentate, long-stalked leaves, 4-8X1,5-4 cm in dimension. The flowers are pink-lilac, in terminal spikes and strongly fragrant.
- **PREHISTORIC MINT:** On the first known scripture of the Greek language (1450 B.C.), that is on clay Linear B tablets, there are frequent mentions of mint. It was one of the herbs kept in the palace store-rooms and used in the preparation of perfumes.

One of the members of the Mint family.

- **MEDICINE:** This herb yields 1% essential oil consisting principally of menthol, which is responsible for its flavouring and refreshing qualities. Hippocrates and Galenus considered it an important herb. Popular medicine utilizes its anaesthetic, carminative, antiseptic, antispasmodic and eupeptic properties, to treat stomach ulcers (gastritis), indigestion, nerve disorders, vertigo, insomnia etc.

- **MINTHE (MINT), A BEAUTIFUL NYMPH**
In ancient mythology Minthe (the Greek ancient name for mint), was a pretty Nymph. A god fell in love with her. It was Pluto, the god of the Underworld. It seems that this love lasted up until Persephone, Pluto's wife, found out and got very angry. She went in search of Minthe, found her somewhere in the mountains of the Peloponnese and started trampling on her. Pluto hurried to rescue her, but only managed to transform her into a beautiful fragrant shrub, mint... Since then this plant is devoted to Pluto...

- **USAGE:** In cosmetics, mint oil serves as an ingredient for scents, soaps, toothpastes and mouth washes. In the pharmaceutical industry, it is used for flavouring mint pastilles and syrups taken against colds, coughs and sore throats. In the preparation of foodstuffs, it flavours fruit salads, particularly with strawberries, sweet preserves, creams, soft drinks and ice-creams. The "marriage" of mint with chocolate requires a special mention. Mint is widely used in the manufacture of syrups and liqueurs. Mint tea is very popular, especially cold, owing to mint's characteristic scent and cool inducing feeling. In cooking, it is used sparingly.

MENTHA PULEGIUM AND THE ANCIENT "KYKEON"

MINT SUBSPECIES: The mint family comprises of many members (more than 20), with insignificant differences among them. The very well known *Mentha pulegium* is among the most widely used...

- **"KYKEON" WITH MENTHA PULEGIUM:** In Eleusis in Attica, an ancient place of worship to Demeter, the goddess of Agriculture, the initiates used to drink a mixture of flour, water and mentha pulegium. It was a kind of holy drink which owed its use to the myth: When the god of the Underworld abducted Demeter's daughter, Persephone, the goddess started looking for her desperately. She neither drank nor ate anything. The earth started to become dry until the other gods interfered, seeking a compromise. They finally found a solution: Persephone would stay 6 months in Hades' underground palaces and the other 6 months with her mother. Demeter broke her fasting and drank "kykeon", flavoured with wild mint. Hence the habit of drinking it, although there are a few versions of this drink (on some occasions, it was a porridge-like dish). There was such a dish made with barley (grains or flour), wine, cheese, honey and mint.

- **"GROUTA" WITH MENTHA PULEGIUM:** "Grouta" was a cheap porridge-like dish, popular in Byzantium, made with roasted flour and water. It was flavoured with wild mint. It may have been a development of the ancient Greek "kykeon". "Grouta" is still made in Greece!

Spearmint (Mentha spicata)
Family: Labiatae

- **HARVESTING:** All year round.
- **DESCRIPTION:** A perennial herbaceous plant similar to peppermint. The difference is in the aroma, its leaves are stalkless, thinner and a little wrinkled and the inflorescences are smaller and thinner. The origin of this species is unknown.
- **MEDICINE:** In antiquity it was a remedy against cholera (it was administered together with sour pomegranate juice) and vomiting. Dioscurides recommended it as a cataplasm for headaches. Its juice healed earaches.
- **AN ANCIENT CONTRACEPTIVE METHOD!** In antiquity spearmint or peppermint was inserted in the woman's vagina after sexual intercourse because they believed that they functioned as contraceptives!
- **FORBIDDEN IN WAR TIME!** During the Middle Ages the generals forbade their soldiers to consume spearmint, because they believed it was an aphrodisiac and provoked... sexual desire. If the soldiers consumed it, they... would get weaker and wouldn't fight vigorously!
- **USAGE:** It flavours soups, salads and sauces. It works well

with pastas, potatoes, lamb, meatballs, tomatoes, eggplants, courgettes, mushrooms, cheese pies and cheese salads. It is the chief ingredient of the popular "mint sauce". The monk Agapius Landus (17th c.) suggested that lentil soup should be flavoured with spearmint.

Savory (Satureja thybra)
Family: Labiatae

• **HARVESTING:** April – July.

• **DESCRIPTION:** A perennial woody hairy short shrub, 20-40 cm tall. Its leaves are narrowly lanceolate to obovate, with a pointed end, 9-14X3-5 mm in dimension. The flowers are mauve, pink or white (8-12 mm), arranged in dense terminal spikes at the tips of the branches. It grows in the eastern Mediterranean, on stony ground, together with thyme, at an altitude of 0-1600 m. In Cyprus another plant is known by this name, the plant *thymus capitatus*, the common thyme.

• **MEDICINE:** It contains volatile oil 1-2 (3,5)%, with carvacrol and thymol (35-38%) being the main ingredients. Its strong antiseptic action is owed to the carvacrol content. According to Hippocrates, it is recommended against lung abscesses, though not against pneumonia and also against female disorders. It was considered an aphrodisiac and for this reason monks were not allowed to have it in their gardens. Its tea is antiemetic and soothes sore throats.

- **"THYBRIOS" APOLLO.** Apollo, the god of ancient beauty, also bore the name of "thybraeos" and "thybrios". The sanctuary of Thybraeos Apollo was in the town of Thybra, close to Troy. The name may echo the local worship of the handsome god.

- **USAGE:** Theophrastus refers to it as "thybra" or "thybron" and according to Dioscurides it was used in the preparation of "thybritis" wine. This application has survived up to our times and sprigs of savory are placed in the funnel through which grape juice (must) is poured into the wine barrel.

According to a reference by Columela, savory flavoured almost every dish in Roman times! Its culinary applications are similar to those of oregano. Savory is the chief flavouring agent for beans, so much so that in Germany, it is called "Bohnenkraut" («bean herb»)!

It is also an ingredient in salads, fish and vegetable soups, dishes with meat or cheese as well as in omelets, bread and fruit salads. It is used in the manufacture of liqueurs and vermouths.

- **BYZANTINE AGHIOZOUMI:** A popular soup was made in the Byzantine times only with onions and olive oil and was flavoured with savory.

It was served over bread crumbs. It was known as "aghiozoumi" (soup of the saints) and was the monks' soup.

Thyme (Coridothymus capitatus)

Family: Labiatae

- **HARVESTING:** Just before and during the flowering period (May to September).
- **DESCRIPTION:** It is a perennial woody shrub, growing to 25-50 cm, with many erect stems branched from the base. In seaside areas or at high altitudes it is found to have a hemi-spherical shape, owing to the trimming by the cold wind. The leaves are narrowly lanceolate, almost smooth, stalkless, 4-10X1-1,5 mm in dimension. The flowers are pink, rarely white, arranged in conical inflorescences like small heads (6X2 mm). It is the chief representative of the woody plants of the Mediterranean areas. It grows on rocky areas, 0-600 m altitude, usually in places close to the sea. On Crete it can be found at higher altitudes, even 1500 m.

The commercial name of thyme is "Spanish oregano". Many people use it in place of oregano because they are similar in scent. It is the herb that attracts bees more than any other.

- **MEDICINE:** Its content in essential oil is (0,5)1,5-2(5)% and the main ingredients are the phenols thymol and carvacrol. It has approximately the same consistency with the ethereal oil of oregano and the same antioxidative and microbicidal qualities. It is a strong antiseptic, expectorant and spasmolytic. It is recommended in cases of respiratory infections, colds, sore throats, tooth decay and fungal infections. In antiquity it was administered as a remedy against asthma, just like today.

• **TUTANKAMUN'S THYME.** A sprig of thyme was found inside Tutankamun's tomb, one of the pharaohs of Egypt.

It had probably been imported to Egypt from other areas in which it grew, maybe even from Minoan Crete with which Egypt had commercial relations.

• **USAGE:** Its pungent scent helps to bring "the great outdoors" to many foods.

Thyme flavours olive oil, pickled olives, butter, vinegar,

meat, poultry, fish, stews, soups, sauces, meat pies or vegetable pies. It is an excellent addition to salads or stuffed vegetables. It also gives flavour to bread, cookies and sweets. It is one of the ingredients of the French mixture "herbes de Provence" and "bouquet garni".

In Jordan and other Arabic countries, thyme is used in "Zahtar" (see recipe further below). In Egypt, another herb mixture is very popular, "dukka", which, apart from thyme, contains coriander, sesame seeds, cumin and pepper and flavours meat or is sprinkled on bread slices, drizzled with olive oil. Alone or in combination with other herbs, it makes a good tea.

In antiquity it was regarded as "a cheap herb" because it was abundant and was consumed by the poor.

Thyme by the sea, Sarakiniko beach, islet of Gavdos.

Caper (Capparis spinosa)
Family: Capparidaceae

- **HARVESTING:** May – August. Not only the tender shoots and leaves but also its buds are harvested.
- **DESCRIPTION:** It is a smooth shrub with spiny creeping branches, up to 1-2 m long (the specific name –*spinosa*- means spiny). The leaves are entire, elliptic or ovate. The flowers are large, white, solitary, with many arched stamens which are longer than the petals. The fruit is a berry, spindle-shaped, many-seeded. The plant is widely distributed in the Mediterranean, it grows wild throughout Greece and particularly in seaside areas.
It can be seen on stony ground, on arable land, on old walls or on rocky slopes.
It has two subspecies, a) *ssp. spinosa* and b) *ssp. rupestris*. The former has ovate-round leaves and the latter elliptic-obovate. The former prefers to grow away from the coastline, on arable land or on road sides, while the latter prefers the seaside rocky areas.

- **MEDICINE:** Ancient physicians used caper widely as a diuretic and for the treatment of sciatica, nervous disorders and other ailments. Hippocrates regarded it as an expectorant and a remedy for the treatment of pleurisy.
Dioscurides, who recommended it against many conditions, quoted that if it is boiled in vinegar and used as a mouthwash, it stops toothache.

- **USAGE:** It has been an edible plant since antiquity. Dioscurides suggested that it should be eaten cooked because that way it was better for the stomach. It seems that it had been known about since prehistoric times. In Athens, during the classical period, it was food for the poor. In texts of later times we read that caper was harvested and kept in brine!
The Monk Agapius Landus (17th c.)

advised people serving it with olive oil, vinegar and raisins or with olive oil, vinegar and honey. Capers are regarded as a very good appetizer. The tender shoots, the flower buds and the young fruits of caper are harvested today and pickled in salt and vinegar. It is used as an ingredient in salads and as a seasoning in sauces for pastas, fish, meat and even pulses. In the Cyclades islands, split-pea purée with caper sauce is a popular dish.

● **THE CAPERS OF THE MOST FAMOUS CONCUBINE!**
Timocles, a satirical poet of the 4th century B.C., wrote that the most famous Hetaira of antiquity, Phryne, picked and sold capers in the market of Athens. An old friend of hers

complained that Phryne shut him out of her house:

> *"I, the unfortunate one, have loved Phryne*
> *since when she was poor and picked capers...*
> *Now she shuts her door and keeps me out of her house!"*

It was connected with poor people in ancient times. In Roman times, its consumption was so high that it was processed inside big barrels with vinegar.
The buds were placed in them and later they were separated into different size buds through large bronze sieves. Wealthy Romans disregarded capers.

Nasturtium (Tropaeolum majus)

Family: Tropaeolaceae

* **HARVESTING:** The flowers are harvested from May to September.
* **DESCRIPTION:** A perennial plant, cultivated for ornament, but also for food and for medicinal purposes. It grows quickly.

The stems creep or climb up to a length of 3 meters. Its leaves are shield-shaped with a black stalk. The shape of the leaves accounts for the generic

name *(Tropaeolum)*, as it was on the shield that the ancients placed the victor's trophies (tropaea). The flowers are large, up to 8 cm in diameter, and have a straight spur. There are many varieties with single or double flowers of flushed yellow, orange or crimson colour, one or many-coloured, dwarf (15-25 cm) or climbing (2-3 m).

It comes from Peru and grows in warm areas, on moderately fertile soil, drained and cool. It is cultivated for ornament, for the beauty of its leaves and flowers, which are unique, but also because it blossoms throughout the summer (May – September).

* **MEDICINE:** Its main active constituent is a glycoside, glucotropeolin, which, when dissolved in water, releases sulphurous by products with anti-biotic powers.

Popular medicine uses it as a disinfectant of the urinary system, for dysmenorrhoea, colds, skin diseases, hair treatment and as a laxative.

• **USAGE:** Not only the leaves, but also the flowers, the buds and the unripe fruits of the plant are utilized.

The fruits and the buds can be pickled in vinegar, just like capers, and are similar in taste and flavour. The young leaves can be used in soups, together with other vegetables, giving a sharp, peppery taste, similar to that of rocket or cress.

The leaves, the shoots, as well as the open flowers which can garnish salads, have a pleasant taste and are regarded as an aphrodisiac.

Coriander (Coriandrum sativum)
Family: Umbelliferae

• **HARVESTING:** The plant flowers in the summer (June – August). The leaves are harvested prior to the flowering period and the seeds when ripe.

• **DESCRIPTION:** An annual herbaceous plant, 20-40 cm tall. It has pinnatisect leaves with linear to ovate leaflets. The flowers are white or pink in terminal umbels, with 2-6 unequal rays 0,5-2,5 cm long. The fruits have alternate wavy and straight ridges. In many countries it almost self-sows, from seeds which escape from cultivated plants. Cilantro, that is the green parts of the plant, has a disagreeable bug-like odour which is not pleasant to everybody. Some

people love it and others dislike it. On the contrary, the fruits have a very sweet smell.

It is a plant of unknown origin, cultivated in many temperate regions, notably Eastern Mediterranean countries, Russia, Northern Africa, South America and India. There are two varieties according to the size of the fruit: one with a small fruit (microcarp, 1,5-3 mm) and one with a large fruit (macrocarp, 3-6 mm).

• **MEDICINE:** Coriander is mentioned in one clay tablet of the Mycenaean period (PY Un 249.1), together with other ingredients intended for ointments. Its fruits are eupeptic, spasmolytic and carminative. In external use they soothe the pains in the joints. Owing to these properties, it is included in the mixture of herbs used for the preparation of *melissa water*, "eau de melisse des Carmes", which was made by a 15th century monastic order of the Latin Church.

Coriander was a widely used herb in antiquity. Hippocrates recommended it as a remedy against hysteria and jaundice. Dioscurides (3,63) cured a large number of diseases with coriander (erysipelas, herpes, anthrax, tumors and skin inflammations). He also advised against consuming large quantities of fruits because they cause mental imbalances.

• **220 MILLION FRUITS!** It was one of the best known herbs of prehistoric times! In Minoan Crete it was cultivated in a systematic way. The annual production was 220 million coriander fruits. Hippocrates informs us that in his time it was eaten "both cooked and raw" (De affectionibus 54,264).

• **USAGE:** Coriander is a popular seasoning, especially in Cyprus. Its fruits flavour soups and other cooked foods, sausages, pickles, creams, cheese salads, bread, biscuits and other flour products. It goes well with kid and lamb but also with pork, particularly when cooked with orange juice.

It is among the ingredients of the Egyptian *falafel* (balls with pulses) and *dukka* (slices of bread sprinkled with roasted and ground sesame seeds, hazelnuts, coriander, thyme, salt, pepper, cumin and olive oil), as well as of the curry mixture. The chopped leaves are used in salads, just like parsley, in sauces, omelets or soups. The essential oil is used as a flavouring agent in the manufacture of alcohol drinks like Gin and Kirsh.

• **IN ANCIENT COOKING:** Athenaeus refers to an interesting dish: hare with coriander. In another chapter he mentions another dish, lentils with coriander! In Epaenetus' "Art of Cookery" (1st c. A.D.), there is note of "myma", a dish made with entrails, tender meat, cheese and plenty of herbs, including coriander.

Lavender (Lavandula angustifolia)

Family: Labiatae

- **HARVESTING:** Both the leaves and the flowers can be used. Leaves are best harvested before the plant flowers. Flowers are best harvested when three quarters of the flower has already bloomed. The whole inflorescences are cut with a small part of the branch.
- **DESCRIPTION:** It is a genus with over 30 species, such as French lavender (Lavandula stoechas) and the hybrid (*Lavandula hybrida*). There is also another genus the main representative of which is lavendin (*Santolina chamecyparissus*). All lavender species are aromatic plants with considerable applications in popular medicine. However, the species used most is the cultivated plant Lavandula angustifolia (Narrow-leaved lavender). It is a multi-branched bushy shrub, 30-80 cm in height. The leaves are linear with short grey down. The flowers are mauve, 10-12 mm, in cylindrical spikes, topped with 1-3 sparse, terminal whorls. It grows wild in the Western Mediterranean but is also propagated by seeds and stems.
- **HISTORY:** The earliest references of this plant occur in Roman writings which refer its use in cooking and as a scent for baths. Besides, the name is derived from *lavo* or *lavare* (to wash, to bathe). It was also used to give a pleasant smell to clothing and linen.
- **MEDICINE:** The Byzantine physician Aetius advised drinking it with water and honey. Galenus prescribed it for the treatment of respiratory infections, headaches and other problems. Popular medicine considers it to be spasmolytic, a tonic, diuretic and disinfectant. It has been used for massaging the skin in cases of skin diseases.
- **"KARABACHI":** Lavender was an ingredient of one of the most popular therapeutic oil

A species of the Lavender genus   *Lavendin*

mixtures that were widely used till the beginning of 20th century. On Crete, its name was "karabachi" and it was used as a lotion.

- **USAGE:** Its essential oil is used in the cosmetics industry for the production of soaps, scents and toilet preparations, so much so that in Southern France, it is cultivated systematically for this purpose. Excessive use of the herb is dangerous for pregnant women, because it stimulates the uterus. Both the leaves and the flowers have ample culinary uses, mainly in confectionery and in the manufacture of beverages, as well as in the preparation of teas. They are also used as a flavouring agent and to enrich the taste of meat, cheese, salads, bread, biscuits, fruit salads etc. Bunches or bags with lavender are kept inside wardrobes and drawers to repel insects and protect or correct the odour of the clothes.
- **LAVENDER WINE!** Although there is no evidence for the use of lavender in prehistoric times, the residue analyses performed with contemporary methods showed that there had been wine inside clay vessels, together with one of the following herbs: lavender, laurel or sage. (Minoan and Mycenaean Taste", Athens 1999, p. 163). Dioscurides (1st c. A.D.) refers to lavender wine (stoechaditis). He considered it a medicine not only for epilepsy, but also for painful ribs and bad nerves.

Lemon verbena
(Aloysia triphylla, Lippia citriodora)
Family: Verbenaceae

- **HARVESTING:** Spring – summer.
- **DESCRIPTION:** It comes from South America and is cultivated as an aromatic-pharmaceutical as well as ornamental plant. It is a shrub, 1-1,5 m tall or more if the soil is fertile. The leaves are dentate or entire in whorls of three or four, lanceolate with a short petiole, smooth above and bearing plenty of glands below. The flowers are white, small, arranged in axillar whorls or in terminal racemes. The leaves emit a lemon scent when touched.
- **MEDICINE:** Popular medicine utilizes lemon verbena for the healing of stomach disorders. Its infusion is believed to be a tonic, antifebrile, diuretic and to stop diarrhoea. It is recommended in cases of nephrolithiasis.
- **USAGE:** Both the leaves and the flowers can be used, however, it should be consumed moderately because it contains camphor. Today it is rarely cultivated and its culinary qualities have almost been forgotten. Due to its strong lemon scent, it can be used to flavour fish, soups, salads, meat and poultry. However, its principal application is in confectionery and in the manufacture of beverages. It is a perfect match to fresh fruits, fruit salads, fruit juices or deserts based on fruit. Dried lemon verbena makes an excellent infusion.

Parsley (Petroselinum crispum)
Family: Umbelliferae

- **HARVESTING:** All year round.

- **DESCRIPTION:** A biennial herb cultivated more for its leaves and less for its seeds. It probably comes from SE Europe and W. Asia and has spread virtually everywhere. It is a herbaceous plant, 40-60 cm tall, smooth with a characteristic smell and taste. The basal leaves are bipinnate or trippinate, with oval, cuneate, trifid segments. The upper leaves are usually trifid with entire lanceolate-linear segments. The flowers are green-yellow in umbels, 8-20 rayed. The seeds are 2,5-3 mm wide, ovoid. There is a variety with curly leaves and another with a root like that of the carrot.

- **MEDICINE:** The whole plant, but mostly the seeds, contains ethereal oil composed of apiol and myristicin. It also contains flavones, vitamins B1, B2, niacine A and C. Vitamin C and A exists in high doses: C, 24 times as much as in lettuce and A, 100 times as much as in cabbage! Parsley is a diuretic, digestive, carminative, expectorant, aphrodisiac and emmenagogic.
Popular medicine utilizes it in dealing with a large number of diseases, principally respiratory infections and conditions of the skin and the eyes.
Dioscurides believed its seeds to be diuretic, emmenagogic and therapeutic for the discomfort of the stomach and the abdomen.

- **"PETROSELINITIS" WINE:** Parsley-scented wine was made in Byzantine times, probably by putting parsley inside the wine barrel, and was used for therapeutic purposes (it was regarded as a diuretic and sleep inducer).

- **USAGE:** Parsley is one of the commonest herbs used throughout the world.
It works well with just about... everything and, due to this fact, there is a saying in Greece, "just like parsley", referring to those who appear everywhere, without a significant role. It is used to give flavour and taste to meat, fish, soups, sauces, salads, omelets, pulses and other dishes. It is the basic ingredient in European herb mixtures, such as "bouquet garni" and "fines herbes".
On Crete, it is also used as a vegetable, in large amounts, in the preparation of delicious dishes, like chicken with parsley.

Ironwort, mountain tea (Sideritis syriaca)

Family: Labiatae

• **HARVESTING:** During the flowering period (May – August).
• **DESCRIPTION:** This plant has 2 sub-species, ssp. syriaca and ssp. nusairiensis. The former is indigenous to Crete, the latter grows wild in Asia Minor and Syria. It is a shrub with almost woody erect stems, 20-50 cm tall. The whole plant is covered by whitish dense hair. The basal leaves are ovate-spathulate, (20-35X7-10 mm) with a stalk 5-10 mm long. The leaves on the stems are linear or elliptic, almost stalkless, (15-50X5-10 mm). The inflorescences are arranged in whorls 5-20 mm long with yellow florets. It grows wild in all mountainous areas on Crete, at an altitude of 1000-2000 m. The herb is almost extinct due to excessive harvesting and animal grazing. Greek mountain tea is confused with Cretan bettony (*Stachys cretica*), because they are so much alike.

It has no relation to "Sideritis" that is mentioned by Dioscurides, who identifies *Stachys cretica* by this name. It contains a small amount of ethereal oil (0-0,2%).

• **MEDICINE:** It can treat ailments of the circulatory system, due to the flavonoids it contains.

Popular medicine recommends it as a diuretic, for the treatment of indigestion problems, colds, coughing and respiratory problems (mountain tea with cinnamon and honey).

• **USAGE:** Sideritis decoction is the most popular tea among the inhabitants of Western Crete.

It is usually mixed with "adonajida" (*Origanum microphyllum*) to improve its taste.

Professor Mich. Defner, who visited Ctrete at the beginning of 20th century, regarded it as very aromatic and warming.

It was offered to him with his breakfast.

Mountain tea. One of the species growing in Greece.

Marjoram (Origanum majorana)
Family: Labiatae

- **HARVESTING:** The leaves and the flowering shoots are harvested during the summer. If the plant is cut at the base before the flowers open, it re-grows and can be harvested again in the autumn.
- **DESCRIPTION:** A multi-branched semi-woody shrub, 30-60 cm tall. The leaves are small, rayed, orbicular or spathulate, with thin grey down. The flowers are small (2-5 mm), white, in elongated spikelets forming terminal racemes. The plant emits a pleasant fragrance, reminiscent of lavender. It grows wild in Cyprus and southern Turkey and is cultivated in many Mediterranean countries and in America. It is regarded as one of the most popular herbs.

- **IN ANCIENT MEDICINE:** Ancient Greeks called the plant "amarakos" and used it for medicinal purposes, against a large number of diseases including female and nerve disorders to name a few. In recent times, singers have drunk marjoram tea to soothe their vocal chords and maintain their good voice. It is believed that it has digestive, antispasmodic and antiseptic properties.
- **THE SCENT OF LOVE:** It was believed in antiquity that the lucky one who happened to meet the goddess of Love, Aphrodite, found out that the beautiful goddess of the Greeks smelled … like "amarakon", that is, like marjoram! In the ancient world, too, it was customary to crown newly married couples, during the wedding ceremony, with wreaths made from fragrant marjoram sprigs.
- **THE PERFUME OF THE ELITE:** In ancient times a famous kind of oil was made, scented with marjoram, the "amarakinon". Athenian ladies liked that perfume so much that when there was a shortage of it, they imported it from Syria!
- **USAGE:** It makes an excellent tea and a perfect seasoning in cooking. It is used in perfumery and in the pharmaceutical industry (its ethereal oil). Marjoram resembles oregano and combines perfectly with tomato and onion dishes, as well as with meat. On the island of Cefallonia, it is an indispensable ingredient in the traditional meat pie. Marjoram flavours fish cooked in the oven, omelets, pasta sauces, salads, green pies, minced meat and sausages. For the Germans, it is the "sausage herb" (Wurstkraut). It can be used in bread making, as well as in the manufacture of beverages. It is one of the ingredients of the well known "vermouth". Marjoram tea is very much appreciated by popular medicine.

Fennel (Foeniculum vulgare)

F. Umbelliferae

- **HARVESTING:** The green parts are harvested at the end of the winter and during the spring (usually from January to May).

It blossoms from June to August, so the seeds are harvested in the summer, as soon as they become brown, just before they fall.

- **DESCRIPTION:** It is a perennial herbaceous plant, smooth with a stem up to 2 m tall.

The leaves are compound, three or four times pinnatisect in the form of thread-like segments. The flowers are small, yellow, in umbels with 10-30 rays of almost equal length. The seeds are 4-8 mm long. The whole plant, as well as the seeds, has a characteristic pleasant smell. The species grows wild in areas around the Mediterranean Sea and has been popular since ancient times.

The self-sowing plant belongs to the subspecies *piperitum* which has a different umbel, with 4-10 rays, and much stronger fragrance than the cultivated fennel. It grows by roadsides and on wasteland throughout Greece.

• **HISTORY:** It is one of the herbs that have been used since time began, notably by the Greeks, the Egyptians and other peoples of the Eastern Mediterranean. It is mentioned on Linear B tablets, the oldest Greek written form of language (1450-1100 B.C.). Then it was used as an offering to the gods! In the classical period, it  flavoured edible olives, a practice which is still popular in many parts of Greece.

• **MEDICINE:** The whole plant contains essential oils composed mainly of anethole (50-60%) and fenchone (20%), which is bitter and sharp.

The seeds contain 10% etherial oil and are used as a tonic, carminative, eupeptic, diuretic, galactagogue and spasmolytic.

In ancient times it was a valuable herb, curing a considerable number of diseases, mostly gynaecological. Hippocrates believed that it facilitated childbirth and Dioscurides thought it facilitated the flow of breast milk.

He also emphasises that it stops nausea and vomiting, as well as any discomfort of the stomach. Moreover, he considers it to be a remedy against the afflictions of the eyes, just as was practised in popular medicine on Crete in recent times. It is also used in popular medicine as a tonic, diuretic, galactagogue and digestive.

• **USAGE:** Fennel is used extensively in cooking, to give a delicate sweetish taste. It goes well with seafood, fish, snails, meat, soups, omelets, cheese salads, cheese pies, vegetables, sauces, rice and pulses. It is an ingredient in mixtures for pies, together with other herbs and vegetables. It can also be used alone in such dishes, such as the Greek fennel pancakes and fennel pies which are excellent preparations. It is employed to flavour tomato paste, pickles, edible olives and olive oil.

Fennel seeds, just like poppy seeds, sesame seeds, dill seeds, anise seeds and celery seeds, impart their sweet aroma to bread, cookies and other pastries.

Florence fennel is grown as a vegetable, mostly for its root, which is consumed either raw in salads or cooked.

• **MEAT WITH FENNEL SEEDS:** In the medieval Orthodox monasteries, fennel added aroma to meat cooked on the grill. Agapius Landus (17th c.) himself advised adding fennel seeds to the meat cooked on the grill.

He also suggested octopus and cuttlefish with fennel (he says that he himself had cooked those dishes many times and liked them). He added that cuttlefish was tastier if cooked in its ink. Another dish mentioned by him was broad beans with fennel or oregano. They are both very popular dishes of his home island, Crete, even today.

Lemon balm (Melissa officinalis)
Family: Labiatae

• **HARVESTING:** In the summer time. The leaves are harvested just before or at the time the flowers appear and are dried immediately.

• **DESCRIPTION:** The plant has three subspecies. It is the ssp. altissima that grows wild in Greece and in most Mediterranean countries. The other two subspecies grow wild in Asia Minor, Syria and Lebanon. It is a perennial herbaceous plant, 40-100 cm tall. The leaves are ovate, dentate (3-10X2-7 cm), with loose hair. The creamy white flowers, 10-14 mm, arched, curved and melliferous are arranged in tight whorls of 6-12 flowers. The currently cultivated plant is the ssp. officinalis, which is more aromatic than the others. It contains very little essential oil (0,01-1%). Russia is the leading country in

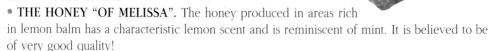

the world in the production of this essential oil, where varieties containing a high percentage of citral (80%) are cultivated. Citral is responsible for the strong lemon scent of the plant.

• **THE NAME:** The generic name of the plant indicates the relation with the lemon and the specific name is an abbreviated form of balsam. The scientific name (Melissa officinalis) denotes the most characteristic properties of the plant: bee plant and medicinal. Not only the flowers but also the leaves attract the bees. For this reason, in many areas new hives are rubbed with lemon balm, to attract swarms of bees!

• **THE HONEY "OF MELISSA".** The honey produced in areas rich in lemon balm has a characteristic lemon scent and is reminiscent of mint. It is believed to be of very good quality!

• **MEDICINE:** It can be used as a remedy against hypertension and depression. It is also carminative, digestive, sudatory and spasmolytic and for this reason it is an ingredient of "melissa water", (eau de melisse des Carmes), which was made by a monastic order of the Catholic Church (Carmes)*, from 17th century. Melissa water is a well known calmative. To make this, flowered lemon balm tops, lemon rind, coriander, cinnamon and cloves are left in white wine for a while.

Dioscurides prescribed fennel against scorpion bites, difficulties in menstruation (in the form of a steam bath with lemon-balm tea), against colic, asthma, arthritis and other ailments. Popular medicine recommends it for skin diseases (even for benign skin tumours), stomach disorders or problems of the mouth cavity.

• **USAGE:** Its lemon scent combines perfectly with dishes which need lemon juice, because it adds extra lemon flavour. Ice cubes containing lemon-balm leaves are a perfect addition to lemonade and other drinks.

It is an excellent match to fruit, consequently to fruit salads and fruit juices. It is one of the herbs mostly used in confectionery and the manufacture of drinks, not to mention that it is an ingredient of benedictine and other herbal liquors.

It is used to flavour a large number of dishes, such as meat cooked in the oven, poultry, fish and soups. It makes a good infusion and is usually served with honey.

*A monastic order of the Catholic Church. It was established in 15th century and its members led austere and laborious lives.

The shepherd's needle, Venus' comb (Scandix pecten-Veneris)

Family: Umbelliferae

- **HARVESTING:** Winter – spring, before flowering.

- **DESCRIPTION:** An annual herbaceous plant, downy, with streated stem, 10-30 cm tall. It bears bipinnatisect or tripinnatisect leaves with linear lobes and white flowers arranged in 2-3-rayed umbels. The mericarps (the combs) bear a beak, 3-4 times longer than them. A plant of the Mediterranean, it grows wild throughout Greece, on arable land or on road sides. There are other species of this plant which grow in stony areas. They are equally aromatic but smaller in size and quantity.

- **MEDICINE:** Dioscurides (1st c. A.D.) states that the plant scandix (there are many members of the same family) is eaten raw but also boiled and aids in the proper function of the intestine, is good for the stomach and acts as a diuretic. He also suggests drinking its tea as a way of healing the liver, the kidneys and the urinary bladder.

- **USAGE:** It is an excellent edible plant with a special taste and flavour. It can be cooked with meat, fish, pulses or it can be an ingredient in pies filled with greens, soups, salads or omelets.

- **FOOD FOR THE POOR:** In some Greek areas, especially in the Peloponnese, it grows in abundance and is used excessively in the kitchen. Probably, due to this fact, it was regarded as the herb of the poor, even in antiquity.

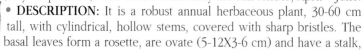

Borage (Borago officinalis)
Family: Boraginaceae

- **HARVESTING:** The flowers are harvested during the flowering period (May –September). The shoots when they are still tender, April – June.
- **DESCRIPTION:** It is a robust annual herbaceous plant, 30-60 cm tall, with cylindrical, hollow stems, covered with sharp bristles. The basal leaves form a rosette, are ovate (5-12X3-6 cm) and have a stalk, 4-7 cm long. The upper leaves clasp the stems and are stalkless. The inflorescences are arranged in terminal leafy racemes. The flowers are bright sky blue, wheel-shaped, five-lobed, about 2,5 cm in diameter and with peduncles 2-2,5 cm long. The stamens have black anthers (3 mm) which are joined and surround the style. The fruit separates into four black, ovate-oblong nutlets with a rough surface. It is a Mediterranean species, grown occasionally for edible and pharmaceutical purposes.
- **MEDICINE:** It contains large quantities of mucilage and vestiges of essential oil. The flowers are emollient while the leaves and the shoots are diuretic. It is a valuable herb for those suffering from rheumatism. It has a beneficial effect on the common cold, bronchitis, scarlet fever and measles. However, it has been principally regarded as an elixir against depression! Popular medicine has utilized a borage infusion against cold and respiratory infections.
- **USAGE:** Both the leaves and the flowers can be used, either fresh or dried, in salads, soups, cold drinks or pickles. Its taste and flavour is vaguely reminiscent of cucumber, so borage combines well with yoghurt and cheese salads. In general, it can be cooked just like spinach. The leaves and flowers can be mixed with spearmint for a wonderful infusion. The flowers can give a characteristic scent and colour to wine and vinegar or can be crystallized and used for the decoration of sweets and pastries.
- **ATTENTION:** The leaves and stems are downy, so only the tender tops are used. This down disappears in cooking.

Alkanet
(Anchusa sp.)
Family: Boraginaceae

- **HARVESTING:** Just like borage: the young tops from April to June, while the flowers from May to September.

The alkanet flowers are often confused with the borage flowers. They are also five-lobed, of almost the same colour, only the inflorescences are different.

Dioscurides states that its leaves brighten the spirit of the drinker when added to wine.

Popular medicine recommends an infusion with its flowers against constipation, rheumatism and anxiety.

On Crete, the leaves are used in pancakes and in Cyprus, the tender shoots are boiled and served with olive oil and lemon juice.

In general, it can be used just like borage.

Oregano (Origanum vulgare & Origanum onites)

Family: Labiatae

- **HARVESTING:** During the flowering period (June – September).
- **DESCRIPTION:** Two different species are known with this name in Greece. The first (O. vulgare) is a perennial, erect, semi-woody at its base, hairy plant, up to 80-90 cm tall. It has multi-branched stems and petiolate, ovate or elliptic, densely hairy leaves. The flowers are white, arranged in terminal corymbs. It grows wild in sunny, rocky places and dry slopes all over the eastern Mediterranean where it comes from. It grows throughout Greece but prefers the dry regions of southern Greece, from the plains to the mountains (0 to 1500 m). It is probably the same as Theophrastus' "White origanum" (Φ, I. 6,2,3) and Dioscurides' "Origanum heracleotikum" (III, 19) which was used

as a seasoning in very ancient times. The oregano eater was called "origanion" (Batracho-myomachia 259).

The second species (O. onites) is similar to the first but its leaves are cordate or ovate with a short stalk. The flowers form larger and denser inflorescences, usually at the top of the main stem. A natural hybrid is usually born from the crossing of the two species in areas where they grow close to each other.

- **SHINING MOUNTAIN!** According to etymological approaches (Zonaras, 12th c.), the word "origanos" is derived from "oros" (mountain) and "ganos" which means splendour, brightness, joy. Consequently, oregano means "shining mountain" or "mountain joy". This can be easily realized if someone visits the Greek mountains, Dicte, Taygetus and others, in June as the place where oregano grows looks like paradise!

- **MEDICINE:** It contains 2-5% volatile oil which is composed mainly of phenols, carvacrol and thymol. Oregano plants from Crete showed a high content of carvacrol (up to 75%) and very little thymol. This oil has antioxitative properties and is used in the food industry as a preservative. It has also been experimentally proved that it is a potent microbicide, due to the high content of carvacrol. In antiquity, it was used for the treatment of a cough (its tea with honey), tonsillitis (its juice) and mouth ulcers. Its tea was also used in therapeutic baths for healing itching and psoriasis. Popular medicine appreciated it as a tonic and eupeptic.

- **HIPPOCRATES' MEDICINE:** Hippocrates, the father of Medicine, recommended oregano in cases of afflictions of the eyes ("eye trichiasis"), toothaches, respiratory problems (lung abscesses), the common cold and female disorders.

• **USAGE:** Both oregano species are excellent seasonings and strong flavourings. It is the most popular herb in different types of cooking. Not only the leaves but also the tops of the plant are used, either fresh or dried.

In Greece, it is mostly used in a dry state but there are some very interesting dishes made with large quantities of fresh oregano, as occurs in the area of Laconia (the Peloponnese), where it is cooked with salted cod fish.

"Ladorigani" is a very popular Greek sauce with olive oil and oregano which flavours a wide range of dishes, cooked in the oven, on the grill or in the casserole. It enhances soups, potatoes, omelets, meat, fish, beans, pastas and tomato dishes. It blends well with basil and is similar in taste and scent to thyme and marjoram.

Celery (Apium graveolens)
Family: Umbelliferae

• **HARVESTING:** The green parts are harvested all year round.

• **DESCRIPTION:** A biennial plant (all biennials quoted here can be cultivated the first year for their green parts, but if intended for seed production, this can occur in the second year). It is a herbaceous plant, 30-100 cm tall, smooth, with a hollow, grooved-angular stem. The leaves are pinnatisect with ovate, cuneiform, three-lobed or trifid leaflets.

The small white flowers are arranged in 6-12-rayed umbels. The fruits are small (1,5-2 mm). It grows wild in seaside regions in Europe, the Mediterranean and South Africa. Currently it is cultivated in variations of two groups.

The first group includes variations cultivated for their green parts, while the second group has variations grown for their fleshy turnip-like root.

• **THE CELERY OF THE HOLY INFANT.** The myth starts with a prophesy: An ancient king in Nemea, in the Peloponnese, named Lycourgos, had a baby son, Opheltis. An oracle from the gods, however, advised Lycourgos not to allow him to set foot on earth until he was able to walk! For this reason he entrusted him to a nanny, Ypsipyle. She never had to let the infant set foot on earth. However, she had to do this once, when she gave water to "the Seven Men" who had travelled from Argos in their campaign against Thebes. She left the infant on a cradle made of wild celery. A snake slithered onto the celery, bit Opheltis and killed him!

It was then that the funeral games were first organized in Nemea, his home town. The champions at those games were crowned with wreaths made with celery. Those games, together with the Pythia, Isthmia and Olympics were the most important games in ancient Greece.

Opheltis today represents the Holy Infant of prehistoric times, the infant that impersonates the young god of Vegetation.

Celery, as the plant of the dying god, was both a plant for the dead and also for the resurrected. For this reason it was planted by graves, symbolizing the resurrection of the dead. Even mourners had celery wreaths on their heads.

• **THE CELERY OF THE COINS.** The word "selinous" has a collective meaning. It signifies the place which is planted all over with celery. In antiquity there were many rivers with this name, as well as a number of towns, the most important of which was situated on Sicily and was a Greek colony. Its coins had a celery leaf on them. It was the holy symbol of the town.

• **MEDICINE:** Both the leaves and the seeds are rich in ethereal oil. It contains antioxidative agents (flavones etc.) and is regarded as a diuretic and beneficial for the function of the kidneys and the urinary bladder.

In ancient Greece it was looked upon as one of the most important aphrodisiac herbs. The physicians of antiquity recommended it in cases of nephrolithiasis, dysuria and kidney diseases (Kassianus Vassus 12, 23, 4). It not only served as a breath freshener but also as a remedy for stomach discomfort and coughing (Dioscurides 3,64).

• **"SELINITIS" WINE.** The Byzantine writer Kassianus Vassus recommended the use of celery-scented wine for the treatment of urinary problems, aches and other complaints. It was made by adding crushed celery seeds into the wine.

• **USAGE:** Although it was known from ancient

Celery on a coin from the Greek city of Selinous (Sicily, 5th c. B.C.). It was the symbol of the city.

times, its culinary use developed much later.

It is mentioned in Linear B tablets (1450-1100 B.C.). Dioscurides states that in his time (1st c. A.D.), it was eaten both raw and cooked. Athenaeus suggests that sea-urchins should be eaten with vinegar, honey, celery and spearmint because, as he says, they are good for the stomach.

Not only the green parts but also the seeds are used in the kitchen, as an ingredient in dishes with meat and fish (pork or dorado with celery are popular Greek dishes) or as a flavouring in soups, salads and appetizers.

In Cyprus, in 19th century, the European Magda Ohnefalsch Richter was surprised to see that it was more often "*cooked with meat than eaten raw in salads*"

(Greek customs in Cyprus, p. 154).

Rose (Rosa sp.)

Family: Rosaceae

- **HARVESTING:** The flowers are harvested in spring, before fully open.
- **DESCRIPTION:** A deciduous or evergreen climbing shrub. The stems are hooked thorns and bear pinnate leaves with dentate or serrate leaflets and winged petiole. The flowers are single or double in many colours and in terminal corymbs with numerous stamens and pistils. The fruit is bottle-shaped, fleshy, bearing many seeds. It is the "rhothi" or "rhothea" of the ancients. Its flower, the rose, has rightly been awarded the title of the king of the ornamental flowers since ancient times and has been the greatest source of inspiration for every artist. No other flower has been praised as much as the rose, from Homer to the contemporary poets.

The species cultivated for their petals are Rosa centifolia (Cabbage rose) and Rosa damascena. (Damask rose). They are both believed to have derived from Rosa gallica (Provence rose) which grows wild in Greece, Asia Minor, the Mediterranean and central Europe. Rosa centifolia is distinguished by its many petals which form a curved cup. They have a characteristic mild scent. Rosa damascena is recognized by its double flowers, of red colour and strong aroma. It is thought to have come from the crossing (hybrid) of Rosa gallica X R. moschata. Rosa damascena blossoms in April – May and it is the species which is intended for rose oil extraction. All the wild species are more suitable for fruit production, but, most of all, Rosa canina (Dog rose). It grows wild on Crete, the Greek mainland, in the other Mediterranean countries and Europe, in shrubby areas and on road or stream sides. It is a shrub, 1-3 m tall, with bowing stems, leaves bearing 5-7 ovate-elliptic, smooth and serrate leaflets and white or pink solitary five-petalled

Rose fruits.
Right: Rose-petal spoon sweet
(the famous Greek rothozachari).

flowers. It blossoms in May – June. The fruit is ovoid, of orange colour, very rich in vitamin C (0,3-1,5%), that is 6-30 times more than in oranges. It also contains flavonoid colouring agents, as well as corotenes (pro-vitamin A). The seeds are believed to be diuretic.

Today a garden without rosebushes is something rare and inconceivable. Owing to its toughness and the existence of numerous varieties, it is thought to be a common plant. An approximate number of 25,000 varieties are currently cultivated.

- **APHRODITE'S FLOWER.** Aphrodite, the ancient goddess of love, was born from the foam of the waves on a beautiful seashore in Cyprus... At that very moment the first white rose was grown on the earth. The other gods wanted to welcome her that way, by offering her a flower with a delicate aroma. They still wanted to send the message of love to the people... Later, when Aphrodite's beloved Adonis was in danger, the goddess ran, barefoot, to save him. Her feet bled and the goddess' blood dyed the rose red! In recent

times it was said that Christ's thorny wreath was made from rose sprigs which are full of thorns. The divine blood ran down and the rose was dyed red.

● **NECTAR AND THE ROSE.** A beautiful myth of antiquity reports that once, the gods were having fun in heaven and were drinking their favoutite wine, nectar. Suddenly, Eros, the permanent partner of the goddess of love, Aphrodite, knocked the wine-bowl with his wing. The nectar flowed from heaven down to the earth... A red rose sprang up on the spot (Kassianus Vassus, 11,17,5).

● **MEDICINE:** The content in rose oil is 0,016%, meaning that 100 kilos of rose petals yield 16 grams of essential oil. Because of its high price, it is blended with geraniol, the essential oil extracted from scented-leaved pelargonium. The infusion or the decoction of the dried petals can be used against diarrhoea, as an astringent. The physicians of antiquity prescribed "rothitis" wine, a medicine prepared by boiling dried rose petals in wine, for curing headaches,

earaches, pains of the eyes, gums, uterus and the intestines. Mashed rose petals were recommended as cataplasms on inflammations of hypochondrium. Especially the mashed petals of the wild rose (Rosa canina) were recommended by Hippocrates as cataplasms on inflammations. In writings of ancient physicians there is plenty of information about the medicinal use of the roses: from curing headaches to treating diarrhoea! (Dioscurides 1,99).

● **USAGE:** Linear B tablets (1450-1100 B.C.) bear the information that at that time there was rose-scented olive oil. Even today olive oil is flavoured with rose petals. The petals can also be utilized for making syrups, jams, essence, "rothosachari" preserve and for flavouring vinegar (triantafyloxido) and wine. Rose water is extensively used in confectionery, in making cakes, cookies and pastries. The fruits are likewise used for jams, jellies, syrups and aperitifs.

Attention: Never use roses treated with dangerous insecticides. Rinse them thoroughly before using.

Sage (Salvia fruticosa)

Family: Labiatae

• **HARVESTING:** April– October.
• **DESCRIPTION:** An ever-green undershrub, 30-80 cm tall, with semi-woody stems and greyish green, downy, lanceolate leaves, bearing two lobes at their base, one on each side, thus making the leaf look three-lobed. The flowers are creamy-white to violet or pink, in a whorl of 2 6 and form a raceme of 10-15 cm. It blossoms from April to June depending on the altitude. It is a woody plant growing wild in waste land, on hills or mountains, (altitude from 50-1000 m), throughout the Eastern Mediterranean and cultivated all over the world.

• **MEDICINE:** The generic name of the plant (salvia), derived from the Latin verb *salvare*, to save, indicates the medicinal value of the herb. It means that it is the "saviour" herb! Its yield in essential oil is 2-4%. Its main constituents are cineol, thujone and camphor. It is an insect repeller. As medicinal, it is used as a cure for a sore throat, headache etc. and is regarded as a spasmolytic, astringent and anti-sudatory. According to Hippocrates, (4th c. B.C.), sage was a remedy for lung diseases and various gynaecological disorders. Dioscurides (1st c. A.D) regarded sage as diuretic, haemostatic and emmenagogic.

Popular medicine uses it for the treatment of a large number of diseases. In fact it is considered almost as a cure-all medicine! It is often used for respiratory ailments, gynae-cological disorders and as an aphrodisiac. In very warm areas of the desert, they drink an infusion of a herb mixture containing mainly sage, believing that it restricts the loss of fluids and prevents dehydration.

On Crete, in times gone by, babies were given a sage infusion with honey to help them fall asleep.

The commonests species of sage (Salvia fruticosa).

A species of the Salvia genus.

As true with all herbs, sage should not be overused, because there have been cases of poisoning.

• **USAGE:** It is used as a condiment and conservative in the food and oil industry. It flavours and offers a pungent taste to poultry, meat, fish, pastas and pulses, added, however, in moderate amounts, because it has a very strong scent.

This is the reason why it should be added in moderate amounts as well, when combined with other, less aromatic, herbs. It makes an excellent tea, alone or in combination with other herbs.

• **A SPOON SWEET WITH SAGE:** A traveller who visited Greece in 1792 was impressed when he saw that they made spoon sweet with sage fruits on the island of Chios! This practice was common in all the Aegean islands, including Crete.

On Crete, too, those fruits were mostly eaten raw and were the children's favourite "fruits". The French traveller Tournefort, who visited Crete in 1700, saw sage fruits being sold at the central market in Heraklion!

> *He unfolded his arm, cut a branch of blossomed sage*
> *and the scent spread and flavoured his mind like mountains.*

> Nikos Kazantzakis, Odyssey Σ 35-36.

Chamomile (Matricaria chamomila)
Family: Asteraceae

• **HARVESTING:** The flowers are harvested from April to June, depending on the area.

• **DESCRIPTION:** An annual herbaceous plant with smooth, erect stems, 10-30 cm tall. The leaves are two or three times pinnatisect, with finely-divided laciniate leaflets. The capitulum looks like a small daisy. The ray florets are ligulate, white in colour. The disk florets are tubular, yellow in colour. The fruits are small achenes, about 1 mm long, subcylindrical, a bit curved. It blossoms in spring and has a pleasant scent. It is a Mediterranean herb growing wild in waste land and on track sides.

• **HISTORY:** The name is derived from ancient Greek *khamaimelon*, "because the flowers give off a scent similar to that of apples", as Galenus writes. That is to say, they are like ripe apples which have fallen down ("*khamai*"). Because of its shape, the ancient Egyptians had offered it to the Sun. In Greece it is also called "Saint George's flower" due to the fact that it blossoms at the time of his celebration (23rd April).

• **MEDICINE:** It is a species that has been used medicinally since prehistoric times and is mentioned by all physicians of antiquity! It is rich in antioxidants (flavones), eupeptic, carminative, anti-allergic and antiphlogistic for skin inflammations or conjunctivitis. The Greek physicians of antiquity recommended it as cure for ailments of the kidneys and the liver, while Hippocrates regarded it as an emmenagogic, when used fresh. This explains the generic name, *matricaria*, from *matrix*, signifying uterus.

Dioscurides states that it rejects the stones from the urinary bladder, sooths abdominal pains, and heals jaundice and mouth ulcers.

Today popular medicine utilizes it as anti-inflammatory for the treatment of skin complaints, wounds, mouth ulcers etc. It is regarded as a perfect sedative and excellent antiseptic medicine.

• **USAGE:** It is used extensively in perfumery for soaps, shampoo preparations for lightening of the hair, creams etc. On the other hand, it has limited culinary use, at least in traditional cooking.

Chamomile is harvested at the same period as mallow (in spring) and a combination of both herbs makes an excellent infusion which is very popular throughout many countries. It has a calming effect and induces sleep. It is also used against colds, upset stomachs and for making eye compresses.

Its use in cooking is very limited. In traditional cooking it is not used at all.

Elder (Sambucus nigra)

Family: Caprifoliaceae

- **HARVESTING:** During the flowering period (May – July)

- **DESCRIPTION:** It is a small, widely spread, deciduous tree. Its leaves are compound, bearing lanceolate leaflets with a toothed margin. The flowers are small, creamy-white, umbel-like corymbs, strongly fragrant. The fruits are small black berries.

The trunk of the tree has a light-coloured, cracked and white-spotted bark. Its branches contain plenty of medulla (this explains its Greek name, *kouphoxilia*). It self-grows on wet, fertile ground, in forests or on the sides of streams and fields.

There is one more species of the plant, *Sambucus ebulus* (Danewort), widely spread, too. It differs from *Sambucus nigra* in the odour, which is absolutely unpleasant.

- **HISTORY:** A plant known from time immemorial, it owes its generic name to the Greek word "*iambyki*" (Hesychius), the Aeolian form of "*sandyx*", meaning red! A red colour was achieved from this plant.

Moreover, it possibly meant the beautiful transparent women's garments, dyed in the colour of the human flesh. "Sambyki" was also a wind instrument, known in ancient Greece, originating from the Orient (Syria or Palestine) and mentioned by a large number of ancient writers, such as Aristoteles, Plutarch and others. It was probably made of wood from the elder tree, from which, in all probability, a weapon was also made.

A medicine is mentioned, too, with this name.

References are not clear and the properties of the tree increased the confusion regarding both its use and its name. In prehistoric times its fruit was used as food, while its flowers were used for medicinal purposes. A magic plant during the Middle Ages, it was connected with a multitude of stories and magic practices.

- **MEDICINE:** Its strong pleasant fragrance is due to an ethereal oil rich in glycosides, tannins etc. and is used as a sudorific and spasmolytic.

Its fruits, which according to Dioscurides smell of wine, contain large amounts of vitamin C. Hippocrates, the father of Medicine, used the plant for the treatment of gynaecological disorders and hysteria. Dioscurides used the crushed tender shoots as cataplasms for gout, inflammations, burns and dog bites.

In general, elder has been used by physicians more than any other herb! Ointments, compresses, creams and many other preparations have been made at times against a range of illnesses, even for the treatment of dandruff and other aesthetic purposes!

At times it was considered a cure-all medicine and all its parts were used, the sap of the leaves, the flowers, the fruits, the bark, even the root. Currently, only the flowers and the fruits are

used, while the leaves, the bark and the root are considered toxic and should not be taken internally.

• **USAGE:** Dioscurides (4,174) informs us that in his time, the leaves were boiled and eaten as a vegetable, for their expectorant properties!

The fruits are eaten or used in confectionery. People in the Caucasus put elder flowers in the wine barrel during fermentation, the Bulgarians make elder vinegar and the Serbians make jams! In the Caucasus, too, they flavour custards with elder.

In general, its principal use is in confectionery, to flavour cakes, biscuits, fruit juices, custard pies and sweet cheese pies. Alone or in combination with other herbs, it makes an excellent infusion that has a calming effect.

Calendula, pot marigold (Calendula officinalis)
Family: Asteraceae

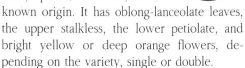

- **HARVESTING:** During the flowering period (April–October).

- **DESCRIPTION:** An annual herb, up to 50 cm tall, of unknown origin. It has oblong-lanceolate leaves, the upper stalkless, the lower petiolate, and bright yellow or deep orange flowers, depending on the variety, single or double.
There is the wild variety as well, the *Calendula arvensis*, with downy foliage. Its flowers look like yellow daisies.

- **MEDICINE:** The essential oil extracted from the flowers contains carotenoid pigments. Medicine has used it for its emmenagogic, healing and anti-inflammatory qualities.
Popular medicine uses it as a disinfectant, antiseptic, as a way of healing the wounds and as a remedy for the ailments of the gastrointestinal system.
On the market there is calendula ethereal oil which is useful for the healing of wounds and burns.

- **USAGE:** The leaves can garnish salads. The flowers (usually dried and ground) give colour and flavour to olive oil, butter, cheese, cheese bread, cheese dips, custards, soups, rice pilaf, pastas and poultry.
In general, it may be regarded as the crocus of the poor. It gives a nice colour to the dish, however not the same taste as crocus.
The flowers, too, make an interesting infusion.

Left: Dr. Zach. Kypriotakis is studying the plants.

Nettle (Urtica pilulifera και Urtica urens)
F. Urticaceae

● **HARVESTING:** January – May. Harvesting should be done with care, better by wearing gloves, because its hairy parts may sting the skin and cause itching and a burning sensation. Only the tender shoots should be harvested.

● **DESCRIPTION:** A very common plant, found almost everywhere, mostly on waste nitrogenous land, in ruined houses or in sheep-folds. It is an annual herbaceous plant with a single erect or branched stem, 20-70 cm tall. Its leaves are ovate, dentate, sharp-ended and the flowers are green, small, on the same spike-like raceme. It is a monoecious plant with unique flowers. It is identified by the stinging hairs which cover the whole plant. Those hairs are long with a pointed end which has a fragile ball, full of substances that may cause itching. As soon as the pointed end pierces the skin, the ball is broken.

● **MEDICINE:** It is a valuable source of metals (iron, silicium, potassium, sulphur, manganese) and chlorophyll. It is actually the main source of chlorophyll sold on the market. The leaves contain formic acid, as well as tannins and vitamins A and C. It has been employed medicinally for its haemostatic, antidiabetic and diuretic qualities.

Hippocrates used it mainly for the treatment of gynaecological problems.

Dioscurides recommended nettle against dog bites, gangrene, cancerous ulcers, nasal haemorrhage, respiratory infections (the infusion taken with honey),

pneumonia, ailments of the mouth cavity and as an expectorant and emmenagogic. He also believed that the nettle had stimulating properties.

Popular medicine has used it against a range of diseases, respiratory, dermatological and gynaecological. A lotion made from nettle is believed to cure eczemas and dandruff. On Crete, in older times, a kind of soap was made from nettle for the treatment of hair and dandruff. It is actually believed to be excellent for the hair!

• **USAGE:** Nettle can be an ingredient in soups and pies. The nettle pies of Thessaly and Epirus are famous! It is usually mixed with other greens and herbs. In general, it can be cooked just like spinach. Nettle can be used in the preparation of pesto in the place of basil.

Spanish oyster plant (Scolymus hispanicus)
Family: Asteraceae

• **HARVESTING:** The edible parts are the spiny leaves (after the spines have been removed) and the cortex of the root. The proper time for its harvesting is the winter and the beginning of spring (January – April), before the flower stem emerges.

• **DESCRIPTION:** A biennial herbaceous spiny plant with an erect-branched stem that can reach a height of 50-80 cm and with spiny and discontinuous stem wings. The leaves are decurrent, spiny, lobed and marbled with white veins. The flower heads are solitary, surrounded by small spiny leaves and the ray florets are yellow. There are many species indigenous to the Mediterranean area and they have a close resemblance to the common thistles.

• **HISTORY:** It has been used as an edible plant since antiquity. The oldest reference is by Hesiod, who defines the seasons regarding the flowering of scolymus as the beginning of summer.

• **MEDICINE:** The root has been used since antiquity as a remedy against various illnesses. Most ancient physicians believed it to be diuretic. They boiled the root in wine and prescribed it for the treatment of dysuria. They also recommended it for the correction of unpleasant body odour. Popular medicine utilizes it for the cure of scores of illnesses: gastrointestinal problems, skin inflammations, nephrolithiasis, arthritis and others. The juice from the boiled roots is considered to be especially therapeutic.

• **USAGE:** Dioscurides (3,14) informs us that in his time they cooked the tender stem, as soon as it emerged, just like the asparagus. The Byzantine lexicographers defined the plant as a vegetable: *"a wild, spiny vegetable"*. It can be cooked alone but also with meat, fish or snails. It can also be made into a pulp and accompany meat dishes.

Artichoke (Cynara scolymus)

Family: Asteraceae

- **HARVESTING:** The leaves can be harvested early in winter and the flower heads in spring and early summer, depending on the region.

- **DESCRIPTION:** It is a perennial herbaceous bushy-like plant, growing to a height of up to 1,5 m with an erect, branched stem which emerges from the center of the plant. Heads are borne at the end of the stems, each consisting of a fleshy part, the choke, which is actually a flattened receptacle before flowering. It is surrounded by involucral bracts that may be either spiny or not. This is the part of the plant that is mostly used for food. The leaves grow from the base and are sinuate pinnately lobed.

- **HISTORY:** In ancient Greece it was not cultivated, unlike Sicily, where it was widely used. On the contrary, "trachia", that is the wild artichoke, was a favourite food of the Greeks and is referred to as a vegetable.
Ptolemaeus the Benefactor, king of Egypt, states that artichokes were grown along the banks of a river in Libya and "the soldiers cut them, removed the thorns, ate them and gave us some to eat as well..." (Athenaeus, 70c).

- **MEDICINE:** It is a remedy for the ailments of the liver and the gastrointestinal system in general (liver failure, jaundice, indigestion). It has been used as diuretic, as well as against skin conditions, anaemia, arteriosclerosis and diabetes.

- **USAGE:** Artichoke is an excellent food. It contains 84% water, 3% proteins, 11% carbohydrates and less than 1% fatty acids. It is a rich source of calcium and various vitamins (A, B1, B2, C). The edible parts are the leaves, the stems (they contain cinarin, tannins, and plenty of enzymes) and the hearts, the chokes, after the thorny leaves have been removed. On Crete, these parts, as well as the tender stems are eaten raw, usually as an excellent accompaniment to "tsikoudia", the traditional alcoholic drink of the island. It can also be cooked in many ways: with meat, fish, snails, broad beans, rice, peas, fennel etc. It can also be pickled or used as an ingredient in an artichoke pie.

Wild artichoke (Cynara cornigera)

Family: Asteraceae

- **HARVESTING:** The leaves are harvested in January – April, before the flowered stem grows. The heads are ready for harvesting in April and May.
- **DESCRIPTION:** A perennial plant, similar to Cynara scolymus, though with smaller and more spiny leaves, of a spreading habit, and smaller flower heads.
- **MEDICINE:** The medicinal value of the wild artichoke was realized in ancient times and was used for healing the complaints of the liver but also as a tonic, cholagogic, even as an aphrodisiac.
- **USAGE:** Although it looks like a sea urchin (it is covered with spines!) and it is difficult to hold in our hands, it is a perfect food for the inhabitants of the Greek islands. In addition to its leaves, which are cooked after the spines have been removed, the heads are also edible, raw or cooked, pickled or preserved in olive oil. They are cooked just like the common artichokes.
- **ANCIENT... ARTICHOKES IN BRINE:** According to Athenaeus (2nd c. A.D.), the leaves of the wild artichokes are consumed, after the thorns have been removed. But, because they are bitterish, they are kept in brine.

This habit, to preserve artichokes in brine, is still in practice, together with the habit of preserving them in vinegar or olive oil.

Black Bryony (Tamus communis)

Family: Dioscoreaceae

- **HARVESTING:** The tender tops of the tendrils are harvested in late winter or early spring.
- **DESCRIPTION:** It is a common herb of Southern Europe, usually found in wet areas, in forest verges or cultivated fields. It is a perennial, tuberous, dioecious, herbaceous climber, with a stem 1-3 m. long. The rhizome is tuberous, spindle-shaped, black on the outer part. The leaves are cordate, acutely pointed, with 5-7 veins (monocoteledons). The flowers are greenish yellow arranged in loose racemes. The fruit is a red berry.
- **MEDICINE:** Although the plants of this family are very toxic, Tamus communis is an edible plant (it is also regarded as a remedy for many diseases), on Crete and in other areas.

Ancient physicians used it for the treatment of female disorders.

Popular medicine recommends it as a remedy for nephrolithiasis and illnesses of the urinary system.

- **USAGE:** On Crete it is appreciated as an excellent vegetable, despite its characteristic bitterness!

The tender tops are used in the kitchen, either boiled (seasoned with olive oil and lemon juice or vinegar) or stewed.

They are also used to make good omelets.

Crocus, saffron (Crocus sativus)

Family: Iridaceae

* **HARVESTING:** The flowers are harvested when they are in full bloom (September – November).

* **DESCRIPTION:** It grows wild in south-eastern Europe and western Asia. It is a perennial, bulbous, herbaceous plant, currently cultivated in a systematic way. Excellent quality saffron is produced in the area of the village of Crocus in the prefecture of Kozani, in Greece. The flowers, 1-2 from each bulb, lilac-coloured and star-shaped, open at night. The stigmas (each plant has three) are orange-red in colour. More than 1 000.000 plants are required to yield half a kilo of saffron.

* **HISTORY:** It was a precious plant in antiquity and there is plenty of archaeological evidence proving its significance. The crocus-gatherer, in the mural from the Minoan palace of Cnossus, depicts an ape picking crocus flowers. Some more wall paintings were found in prehistoric Santorini. The harvesting of crocus seems to be a job of ritual character. It was an official celebration in the Minoan world which probably connected the harvest of crocus with the ritual passing from childhood to adolescence.

The crocus-gatherers depicted in the wall paintings are beautiful young ladies, in festive attire and exquisite jewellery! The crocus harvest was associated with the Great Mother, the Mother-Goddess of the prehistoric world, to whom they offered the annual production.

The role of the crocus has always been multifold: it has been used as a condiment, medicine and a precious dye, which was used to dye the most beautiful clothes in the ancient world. It is not therefore accidental that it is mentioned by all ancient writers.

It seems that those participating in the symposiums of the ancient Greeks, had wreaths from various flowers on their heads. Crocus was among those flowers! They believed that wreaths with crocus flowers induced serene sleep (Plutarch, Quaestiones convivales 647d).

* **"CROCUS-VEILED" EOS.** Homer, the great epic poet of antiquity, used to refer to Eos (the personification of the dawn) as the crocus-veiled: her veil had the colour of the crocus. A poetic image of exquisite beauty, flattering both the dawn and the crocus!

* **MEDICINE:** The stigmas of the flowers contain crocin, a carotenoid pigment. It is so potent that it can dye water even in solution of 1:100.000! In large quantities (meaning a few grams), the stigmas are very toxic. Crocus has been used in Medicine for 3000 years. Hippocrates (4th c. B.C.) recommended it for the

treatment of both old and recent wounds, for ulcers of the genitals and other ailments. Dioscurides writes that it has emollient, digestive and diuretic qualities and that it prevents getting drunk and runny eyes (when mixed with milk). It is recommended for cataplasms for the uterus and the anus. However, from that time they knew that it was fatal if used in large amounts!

• **USAGE:** In antiquity it flavoured wine. In the Byzantine times it had a significant place in the kitchen; "crocomageria" (dish with saffron crocus), was a well known dish mentioned by the Byzantine writers.

It is one of the finest seasonings! It gives colour, taste and flavour to a range of dishes, soups, rice pilafs, custards, cheese, poultry, pastas, bread, biscuits and sweets. There are a couple of herbs that can give a similar colour (calendula, turmeric), neither of them, however, can give the taste and aroma of saffron crocus.

• **"OXYMELI" WITH CROCUS:** The monks on Mount Athos used crocus as a medicine and as a condiment. In one monastery, a recipe of 15th century has been found which gives instructions on how to prepare "oxymeli", that is a dressing with honey, vinegar, dill and saffron crocus.

Mastic tree, Lentisk (Pistacia lentiscus)
Family: Anacardiaceae

• **HARVESTING:** December – January.
• **DESCRIPTION:** An aromatic resin-bearing shrub or small tree, 1-7 m tall. It is a dioecious plant, with compound leaves bearing leathery, shining, deep green leaflets.

The flowers are unisexual, in spike-like racemes. The fruits are small, red, turning black when ripe.

• **MEDICINE:** Hippocrates regarded lentisk as a remedy for gynaecological disorders (cervical ulcers) and hysteria. Dioscurides believed it to be an astringent and recommended it against haemoptysis, diarrhoea and dysentery.

Its resin (and especially of the variety that produces mastic on Chios) was regarded by Dioscurides as a cure for stomach complaints. Today, physicians have studied the qualities of the mastic and have come up with very good results!

In older times, an ointment was made in Crete from lentisk juice and wild onion (Urginea maritima) for the treatment of hair loss. In popular medicine the bark of lentisk has a soothing effect on wounds. The oil produced from the lentisk fruits has been a traditional remedy for curing otitis and some skin ailments, mainly

Harvesting mastic on the island of Chios in 17ᵗʰ century.

eczemas. The resin has been used for the cure of stomach ulcers.

• **USAGE:** The fruits are used as flavouring in foods. The traditional bread on a few Aegean islands and in Cyprus contains lentisk seeds.

They are also used in the sausage industry. The mastic of Chios has ample uses in confectionery, bread making and cooking.

Terebinth (Pistacia terebinthus)
Family: Anacardiaceae

• **HARVESTING:** When the fruits are fully ripe, September – October.

• **DESCRIPTION:** A relative plant of the mastic tree. Its compound leaves are imparippinate, while lentisk's are parippinate. Moreover its inflorescences are much longer. The fruits are similarly red, but they become dark blue when ripe. In winter, and after insect biting, they produce specific galls which were utilized by the Byzantines for dyeing their silk clothes: they give a nice, bright green colour.

• **MEDICINE:** Dioscurides (1,71) believed the terebinth fruit to be an excellent aphrodisiac when accompanied by wine. In older times there was actually wine flavoured with terebinth fruits! The resin produced by

the terebinth tree was used in antiquity (Dioscurides 1,71) as a remedy against coughs, tuberculosis, infection of the lower respiratory system, leprosy, itching of the female reproductive organs, overfatigue and other ailments.

• **USAGE:** The fruits are eaten raw or are added to bread and pastry for flavour.

In Cyprus the tender shoots of the tree can be pickled in vinegar. They can also be fried or used to make omelets.

• **THE "MOUTES" OF CYPRUS:** In the area of Ammochostos in Cyprus, before the Turkish assault in 1974, the people there used the tender sprigs of the lentisk, the terebinth and the savory in cooking. They were regarded as excellent, aromatic food.

A popular Cypriot love rhyme praised the beauty of a young lady by saying that her mother used to eat those tops before she gave birth to her.

Mallow (Malva nicaeensis)

Family: Malvaceae

• **HARVESTING:** The flowers are harvested during the flowering period, (April –July), the tender green tops from December to April.

• **DESCRIPTION:** It is an annual, downy, herbaceous plant, 70-120 cm tall. The leaves are semi-round, slightly cordate. The petals are smooth, 10-12 mm long, light lilac, without nerves. The more common mallow, *M. sylvestris*, has the same usage as *M. nicaeensis*. It differs in the fact that it is biennial or perennial and its leaves have varied shape. They are usually palmate with 3-7 lobes. The petals are 12-30 mm long, pinkish-purple, with dark nerves.

• **HISTORY:** It is a herb much appreciated since ancient times as an edible species. It seems that not only its leaves and tender tops were eaten but also the roots. The Byzantine commentators on Hesiod, the poet who was the first to mention mallow in 7th century, inform us that in very ancient times a nutritious pulp was made from mallow in combination with other plants. In ancient Greece, it was among the plants grown in the gardens. They believed that it staved off hunger and thirst (Athenaeus 58f).

As a very common herb, it was mostly consumed by the common people.

• **THE MALLOW OF THE ANCHORITES:** Epimenides the Cretan, a historical or mythical person, the man who was believed to "have slept" for 50 years in a Cretan cave and was found in a new world when he woke up, was associated with mallow from antiquity: To combat his hunger and thirst, that first anchorite in history ate bulbs and mallow.

It seems that mallow has been the plant of mystic practices and initiations since then. It was particularly favourite among the Pythogorians and was considered sacred (Porphyrius 41), because of the fact that its flowers always face the sky.

According to Iamblichus, Pythagoras suggested avoiding it because it is the first messenger of the "affection" of the heavenly for the earthly (Pythagoras' Life 24, 109).

• **MEDICINE:** Hippocrates prescribed cataplasms with mallow (in wine) for the treatment of swellings and inflammations and its infusion for various gynaecological complaints. Diphilus of Siphnos states that it helps in cases of inflammation of the kidneys and the uterus. It has been used as an expectorant and laxative.

The infusion made from its flowers is recommended for the ailments of the digestive and the urinary system. Popular medicine regards it as a potent medicine against constipation, a property

which is emphasized by the Byzantine writer Symeon Seath. In another Byzantine text ("Anonymi medici: De alimentis"), it is referred to as an excellent digestible food. In Byzantine "Geoponica" (Vassus, 12,12) we read that it cures "the secret passions of women", the diseases of the liver and the kidneys, wounds and many other complaints.

• **"IT COMBATS THE PANGS OF LABOUR"!** For the physicians of antiquity mallow was a precious herb because it served in the preparation of vaginal suppositories which were administered to combat the pains of labour and facilitate childbirth (Hippocrates, De mulierum affectibus 2, 196).

• **USAGE:** The edible parts of the plant are the leaves, the tender sprigs and the flowers.

The green parts can be either boiled or stewed in different ways (they combine perfectly with pulses, meat and rice and with eggs for making omelets). The flowers make an excellent infusion, usually in combination with chamomile.

Rock samphire (Crithmum maritimum)

Family: Umbelliferae

• **HARVESTING:** April - July.

• **DESCRIPTION:** A perennial Mediterranean fleshy plant. The stems and the leaves are glaucus and the flowers are yellowish-green arranged in umbels made up of 8-36 rays.

It grows on the rocky shores of the Mediterranean Sea and the European Atlantic. Dioscurides' description (2,129) is very characteristic: "It is a shrubby herb, of a spreading habit, reaching a height of up to one pecheus (46 cm). It grows near the sea, bears many shining glaucous leaves, like purslane's, however a little broader and longer, and has a saline taste…"

• **MEDICINE:** It has been used as a diuretic since Hippocrates' time (4th c. B.C.)! That significant physician of antiquity recommended it as an emmenagogic, just as other physicians did after him. It is regarded as a detoxifying herb.

• **USAGE:** Both the young stems and the leaves are harvested and preserved in brine. This practice is very old. It is recorded by Dioscurides: "It is used either cooked or raw and is preserved in brine" (1,129).

It can be used as an ingredient in salads. Both the green parts and the flowers can be fried or used to make omelets.

Rock samphire (Crithmum maritimum) on Drapanias beach, Kissamos, Crete.

Dandelion (Taraxacum sp.)

Family: Cichoriaceae

• **HARVESTING:** January – May.

• **DESCRIPTION:** A genus with approximately 2000 species all growing in temperate areas, particularly in well manured fields, but also on paths and wasteland. It is a perennial, herbaceous plant with a carrot-like root. The leaves are oblanceolate, multifid, entire or with a toothed margin. They all surround the root like a rosette and there is no visible central stem but many scapes, 15-35 cm long. They have no leaves and bear terminal inflorescences (heads). The florets are all ligulate, yellow. When it is cut, some white latex is spilled. The fruits are achenes bearing a beak and a white umbel like pappus, which is easily carried by the wind.

• **MEDICINE:** All the parts of the plant have been used medicinally at times, against a range of ailments. The root and the latex contain tannins and other valuable substances. It is regarded as an important source of potassium, an excellent diuretic, cholagogic and detoxifying plant. Popular medicine recommends it in cases of the presence of stones in the gallbladder or in the kidneys.

• **USAGE:** It is a valuable edible plant. In some Greek areas its root (roasted and ground) was used in older

times for the preparation of a coffee substitute. It is excellent as a salad ingredient or cooked like other greens. It has a slight bitterness which can be reduced by boiling and discarding the water. It can be boiled or cooked in tomato or egg-lemon sauce, together with meat or fish. Its flowers can be used in beverages together with lemon or orange juice.

Tassel hyacinth (Muscari comosum)
Family: Liliaceae

- **HARVESTING:** The bulbs are harvested from January to May.

- **DESCRIPTION:** A perennial bulbous plant. The part that grows above the earth is a stem bearing many small bluish-purple flowers. It can reach a height of about 20-30 cm.

It should not be confused with star-of-Bethlehem (Ornithogalum sp.) which, too, is a bulbous plant.

- **MEDICINE:** It has been acknowledged as a pharmaceutical plant since antiquity.

Hippocrates recommended it against the interruption of the flow of the breast milk and the haemorrhaging of the uterus. He also believed that it helped women conceive.

Dioscurides records that cataplasms made with tassel hyacinth are beneficial for the stomach, as well as for sprains, gout and pains in the joints. He still records that the bulbs, either alone or in combination with other herbs, have a healing effect on skin spots, haemorrhoids, sunburn, dandruff and other conditions.

- **APHRODISIAC BULBS:** Even from antiquity it was believed that bulbs cause sexual desire and excitement.

This belief was maintained for thousands of years! The Byzantine physicians and writers as well as popular medicine of 19th century had the same opinion!

- **USAGE:** It has been an edible plant since antiquity! It is surprising that in Greek cooking the bulbs have been used in exactly the same ways for thousands of years: boiled and seasoned with vinegar, as Dioscurides states (2,170).

Their flowers are used in making omelets.

The other bulbous plants

Many bulbous plants of the liliaceae family are generally used both as medicine and as food. The most characteristic examples are the following:

Allium cepa (onion)
Allium sativum (garlic)
Allium schoenoprasum (chives)
Allium porrum (leek)
Asparagus sp. (asparagus)
Ornithogalum sp. (star-of-Bethlehem)

Chives (Allium schoenoprasum). Below: Asparagus.

The first four (onion, garlic, chives and leek) are the most popular seasonings with extensive use in the kitchen (in salads, cheese dips, soups, omelets, pies and casserole dishes). They have been used since prehistoric times.

The Greek emigrants from the area of Alatsata in Asia Minor make a very interesting pie with the flowered stems of the onion.

Star-of-Bethlehem has the same culinary uses as tassel hyacinth (*Muscari comosum*), however it should be used in moderate amounts as it is toxic when used excessively. The flowered stems of *Ornithogalum nutans* are

Onions at the time of flowering.

Star-of-Bethlehem (Ornithogalum sp.)

picked in Crete and make excellent omelets, often together with the stems of tassel hyacinth. The cultivated asparagus (of which there are more than 300 species!) are a rich source in folic acid, have a sweetish taste and are used as ingredients in soups, appetizers, salads and soufflés.

They can also be cooked with meat in egg-lemon sauce.

☞ **Attention!** *Not all bulbous plants are edible! On the contrary, some of them are very toxic.*

A characteristic example is **Colchicum** *which, in very limited doses, has significant pharmaceutical use. Colchicine, a medicine against uric arthritis, is made from Colchicum.*

Wild and cultivated asparagus.

Myrtle (Myrtus communis)

Family: Myrtaceae

- **HARVESTING:** The fruits are harvested in autumn and in winter after they have matured.
- **DESCRIPTION:** A multi-branched plant in the form of a shrub or a small tree, 1-5 m tall, with ovate-lanceolate, smooth, dark green and shiny leaves. The flowers, solitary, fragrant, white, stem from the leaf axils and have five sepals, five white petals and numerous stamens. The fruits are berries, small, spherical, white or black or blue-black. It is a species of the Mediterranean regions.
- **APHRODITE'S MYRTLE TREE.** It was a sacred plant in antiquity associated with several gods but especially with Aphrodite, the goddess of love.

That beautiful   goddess was born

from the foam of the waves, where the sperm of her father (Cronus) had fallen, near the city of Paphos in Cyprus. She came out of the sea and ran to hide behind a myrtle tree. It has been considered her sacred plant since then!

The myths of the ancient world associated with the myrtle are abundant! It is said that the goddess Athena transformed her dying friend Myrsini into a shrub... It was used by ancient people for garlands and coronets, while the famous jewellers of antiquity manufactured exceptional jewels in the shape of myrtle leaves and fruits. A marvellous gold myrtle wreath was found in the Macedonian royal tombs of Vergina, in Northern Greece.

• **PHAEDRA'S MYRTLE.** The plant was also connected with the erotic agony of Phaedra, the mythical daughter of Minos, the king of Crete. As she observed Hippolytus, her husband's son, taking his physical exercise, she desired him so much that she pierced a myrtle leaf with a needle that she had with her!

If you observe a myrtle leaf against the sun, you will think that it is full of little holes. In fact they are the oil bearing glands of the plant.

Right: A myrtle leaf. The oil-bearing glands are visible as white spots. People in the ancient times believed that they were the tiny holes that were made with Phaedra's needle.

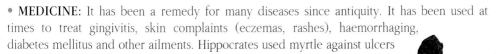

- **MEDICINE:** It has been a remedy for many diseases since antiquity. It has been used at times to treat gingivitis, skin complaints (eczemas, rashes), haemorrhaging, diabetes mellitus and other ailments. Hippocrates used myrtle against ulcers of the female reproductive organs and its essential oil in cases of fainting, against earaches, hysteria and pains in the uterus.
- **USAGE:** People in the ancient world used myrtle to flavour wine ("myrtinitis wine"), or olive oil ("myrtinon oil"). The berries can be eaten raw and make perfect jams. The leaves or the fruits are used for flavouring meat, game, sausages, fish, cheese, cheese pies, liqueurs, wine and dried figs. Meat or fish can be cooked in the oven on a layer of myrtle leaves or the leaves can be used to place cheese pies on them as soon as they are taken out of the oven. They get a fine flavour.

Sorrel (Rumex sp.)

Family: Polygonaceae

- **HARVESTING:** From January to April.
- **DESCRIPTION:** The members of this family are perennial herbaceous plants with a sour taste. The leaves are lanceolate, ovate or arrow-shaped. The flowers, without petals, are green or pink, arranged in racemes. The fruits are ovoid or triangular, in large numbers. In Greece there are 25 species and 11 hybrids, most of which are edible. They grow wild in damp and shady places.
- **MEDICINE:** Doctors in ancient times used it for massaging the abdomen and its roots against leprosy. Popular medicine uses it for a range of conditions (diarrhoea, anaemia, diabetes, hepatitis etc.).
- **USAGE:** It can add taste and flavour to pies, soups, salads, stuffed vegetables and can be cooked as a vegetable with meat in egg-lemon sauce.

Poppy (Papaver rhoeas)

Family: Papaveraceae

- **HARVESTING:** Late winter and spring time (January – May).
- **DESCRIPTION:** An annual herbaceous plant with an erect multi-branched stem and pinnatisect leaves with a toothed margin. The flowers are red. There are many species differentiated by the special characteristics of the leaves, the flowers and the fruit, which is called pepper-pot capsule. It blooms in spring.
- **MEDICINE:** All species of this family have been noted since antiquity for their medicinal values. The Opium poppy (Papaver somniferum) has been associated with Demeter, the goddess of Agriculture, and the periodic sleep, somnis, (it symbolized the death and resurrection of Persephone, who stayed 6 months on the earth and the other 6 months in the underground palaces of Hades). A sleep-inducing drug, it was connected with worship and the goddess of prehistoric Crete, in her representation as the goddess of Medicine. It has been used for thousands of years as a sleep-inducer, calmative and sedative. Flowers of the poppy (P. rhoeas) were used on Crete to make "kokkinolatho", which was therapeutic. Poppy petals were placed in a bottle full of olive oil and left in the sun until the oil turned red.
- **USAGE:** The edible species used in the kitchen is the common poppy (P. rhoeas). Its petals make excellent teas and its seeds delicious sweets. The seeds have been sprinkled on bread since antiquity! Their use has been noted since 7th-6th c. B.C. In Roman times the poppy seeds were roasted and eaten with honey! They were also the chief ingredient in "pasteli" (a sweetmeat made chiefly from honey and seeds), in the place of sesame seeds. Currently poppy seeds are used in bread, cakes, biscuits and pastas. The green parts are cooked with rice or meat and can make omelets and pies, mixed with other herbs and vegetables.

Above: On Crete children make small dolls (koutsounes) with the poppy buds. This is why the plant is called koutsounatha in Greek...

Garden rocket (Eruca sativa)

Family: Cruciferae

- **HARVESTING:** All year round.
- **DESCRIPTION:** A very common perennial herbaceous plant of the Mediterranean flora. The leaves are lanceolate, stalkless, on the tender stems of the top. The flowers are white, cruciform, with red streaks. It can reach a height of up to 70 cm. In addition to growing wild, it is cultivated, too, consequently it is available at any time of the year.
- **A POTENT APHRODISIAC!** Dioscurides states that in antiquity the rocket seeds were sprinkled on boiled green salad! He also notes that when rocket (the green parts as well as the seeds) is consumed excessively, it is a strong aphrodisiac. The seeds were

thought to be a digestive, diuretic and helped in the functioning of the intestines. As it was such an important medicine, it was mashed, mixed with milk or vinegar and given the form of tablets, so that it could be preserved for a long time.

• **A PAIN KILLER:** In Roman times it was used as a pain killer. Those who were to suffer the punishment of whipping (flagellation) were given a glass of wine to drink into which they had soaked rocket. Thus the pains were more bearable!

• **USAGE:** Its pungent taste makes it perfect as an ingredient in salads (it is rather... a modern salad herb). It can also be combined with other vegetables for soups and can be used in pesto sauces in the place of basil.

Perforate Saint John's wort (Hypericum perforatum)
Family: Hypericaceae

• **HARVESTING:** May - September.

It is a widely spread perennial herbaceous plant, with stalkless, small, oblong leaves and inflorescences of yellow flowers.

It is Dioscurides' "askyron", which he used for the healing of burns. He, too, observed that it "smells like resin". Its name, Saint John's wort, is due to the fact that it blossoms on the day of Saint John's celebration (24th June). It has no culinary usage. On Crete, they flavoured olive oil with Saint John's wort and used it for the soothing of wounds and burns. Today it is administered as an anti-depressive medicine, but only with a doctor's prescription.

Small-leaved linden or lime (Tilia cordata)
Family: Tiliaceae

• **HARVESTING:** The flowers and the tender leaves at the tops of the stems are the parts commonly used. They are harvested during the flowering period (June-July).

• **DESCRIPTION:** A common deciduous tree in the European forests, up to 35 m tall. It sheds its leaves in winter, which are alternating, cordate, smooth, dark green above and grey green below. The flowers are small with ivory white petals.

• **MEDICINE:** Its infusion has anti-spasmodic, sudoriferous, expectorant and sedative properties. It is usually drunk before going to bed because it is relaxing.

• **USAGE:** It has no culinary use. Its infusion, however, is an excellent aromatic tea, pleasant tasting and thirst-quenching.

Perforate Saint John's wort.

Linden leaves and flowers.

A linden tree (Tilia cordata) at the monastery of Crysopighi, Chania, Crete.

Miscellaneous herbs

The number of herbs is unlimited! Some of them are intended only for medicinal use, others have additional gastronomic applications.

Salsaly or vegetable oyster (Tragopogon sinuatus), has a wide usage in popular medicine (as diuretic, against nephrolithiasis or cholelithiasis), but is also a tasty herb, which combines very well with other herbs and vegetables in making green pies!

The same applies to **Smooth saw thistle** (Sonchus oleraceous), which is regarded by popular medicine as a cure for numerous illnesses, but is also an exceptionally tasty herb. The species of the **Cichorium** family are extensively used in the kitchen, such as **Black mustard** (Sinapis alba), **Ivory-fruited hartwort** (Tordylium apulum), **Garden cress** (Lepidum sativum), **Tarragon** (Artemisia dracunculus), **Lovage** (Levisticum officinale), **Chervil** (Anthriscus cerefolium), **Caraway** (Carum carvi) and many others.

Cistus creticus is used only in popular medicine and its aromatic resin for specific applications. **Spanish broom** (Spartium junceum) is likewise used in popular medicine and is regarded as a cordial, which should only be taken with a doctor's prescription. Long ago, olive oil was flavoured with this herb and was believed to be therapeutic (it should be noted, though, that its fruits are toxic).

In addition, other herbs exist which are intended only for teas, either therapeutic or not (e.g. **Helicrysum**). **Teucrium capitatum** is such a herb, which has an excellent, strong fragrance

Salsaly or vegetable oyster in blossom.

Helichrysum sp.
Left: Smooth saw thistle (Sonchus oleraceous)

Spanish broom (Spartium junceum)

Chicory in flower (Cichorium intybus)

and was very often used for teas in the past. Today its use is limited, because it is toxic in excessive amounts.

EXPERIENCE IS OUR ALLY!

Nevertheless, there are still herbs that others have tried and adopted for culinary use, which we do not use. In general, the uncommon herbs should be consumed with caution!

There are poisonous plants in nature which are not known to everybody.

Only the specialists in the area can identify them, those who have been using them relying on the experience of many centuries!

CULINARY USE OF
herbs

Herbal beverages

Herbal beverages were known in ancient Greece, long before common tea became popular. Greeks drank herbal teas or tisanes made from wild herbs. At first they were used for medicinal purposes prescribed by ancient Greek doctors, but later they became popular as refreshing drinks as well as herbal remedies. Herbal teas can be relaxing (chamomile, linden, marjoram or lemon-balm tea), refreshing (peppermint) or invigourating (thyme, sage).

There are various methods of tea preparation:

INFUSION: It is the commonest way of preparing tea from herbs. It is suitable when only the leaves and flowers are utilized: Put the water in the kettle and bring it to the boil. In a tea-jug place 1 tablespoon fresh herbs or 1 teaspoon dried herbs for every cup of infusion and pour as much boiling water as required over the herbs. Cover the tea-jug and let the herbs steep for 5-10 minutes depending on the herb or mixture used. Strain through a very delicate cloth or sieve and serve the infusion. It can be kept for one day in the refrigerator and drunk either hot or cold.

DECOCTION: This method makes it possible to extract the useful substances from the tough, woody parts of the plants, roots, sprigs or bark. Since these parts need longer boiling to release their active ingredients, they are mixed in the suitable proportion with water, brought to the boil and kept on a low flame for at least 15 minutes. One teaspoon of dried herb or 1 tablespoon of fresh is used for every one and a half cups of water so that one cup of tea is left after the boiling. For better results, the herb can be chopped up so as to increase the surface in contact with the water and get the most of the active substances. Strain as above and serve.

 MACERATION: It is made by soaking the herb in water, at about room temperature, for 2-12 hours.

A traditional herb distillery at the Lychnostatis museum (Chersonissos, Crete).

 TINCTURE: It is the alcoholic extract of herbs. Put 1 cup of herbs in a container and cover with ½ liter spirit solution (ratio of spirit to water, 1:4. You can use slightly diluted tsikoudia, vodka, rum etc). Place the container in a warm place (about 40° C) and leave for 15 days shaking the container once or twice daily.
Finally strain through thick gauze and store in a dark, airtight bottle. Alcohol acts as a preserver and the drink can be kept for up to 2 years.

 DISTILLATION - THE ESSENTIAL OILS: Distillation is the method used by the traditional herb pickers for the extraction of the essential oils contained in herbs. There are various techniques all based on the same idea: The receptacle (distiller) containing the suitable parts of the herbs (blossoms, leaves or fruits) is heated and the volatile essences are first evaporated and then condensed in a suitable coolant, usually water. Finally the water and oil are separated and the ethereal oil is collected as the product of distillation. Today new methods of ethereal oil extraction have been developed.

 THE TRADITIONAL PERFUMERS
Although distillation is believed to be a relatively new technique, research carried out recently found out that traces of distilled liquids were discovered in Minoan pots!
Many small distilleries existed in the past on Mount Athos, Epirus, the Peloponnese, Crete and the other Greek islands. In the village of Kavoussi in the area of Hierapetra, systematic distillation was carried out until recently, notably of oregano, wild mint, myrtle, sage, laurel, thyme and cedar fruits.
According to the last owner of a distillery, A. Tsourakis, the processing was performed as follows: The herbs were harvested at the end of the flowering period and were dried out in the shade. Then they were put in a cauldron holding 40 lt of liquid, pressed to hold as much as possible, together with 16 lt of water. The herbs were heated in the cauldron, the steam, carrying the various oils, was liquified and collected in the condenser. The ethereal oil, unable to mix with water, forms a layer above it. Specifically for cedar oil, the fruits were

harvested and then crushed to facilitate the release of the ethereal oil.

The yield of each distiller was 600 grams sage oil and 80-100 grams oregano oil, mint oil or cedar oil.

The traditional perfumers of Kavoussi recommended their oils as a medicine against a range of diseases, such as:

- **Cedar oil**: They believed it was the best cure for skin infections, stomach complaints (a few drops in a cup of water), haemorrhoids, etc.

  - **Sage oil:** It was not taken internally, it was only used for massage, to soothe skin inflammations or respiratory complaints.

- **Oregano oil**: It was used against toothache.

- **Mint oil, as well as oregano oil:** They were believed to be beneficial for respiratory diseases.

ꙅ OUZO

The traditional Greek ouzo is an alcoholic extract scented with anise. Apart from anise, fennel, coriander, star anise, dill or mastic are also used as flavouring agents. The secret of success for the Greek ouzo lies in the combination of herbs (seeds), but also in the amount used. An average 50-60 grams of aniseeds are required for each liter of spirit.

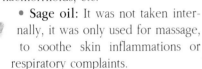

ꙅ CITRON ALCOHOLIC DRINK FROM NAXOS

The citron alcoholic drink from the inland of Naxos in Greece is unique. It is produced in

Citron distillery in Chalkio, on the island of Naxos (it has been run since middle 19th century.)
Below: The traditional alcoholic drink of Naxos.

the traditional way even today.

The ethereal oil of citron is extracted through distillation of the leaves of the tree, together with alcohol. There is also citron liqueur which contains sugar.

ꙅ GIN

Gin is an alcoholic drink flavoured with cedar fruits.

Herbals Teas

The herbs suitable for infusions and decoctions are: **dittany, ironwort (sideritis), chamomile, mallow, lemon balm, lemon verbena, sage, thyme, savory, marjoram, basil, anise, angelica, bay laurel, elder, fennel, hyssop, spearmint, peppermint, rose and rosemary.**

You can prepare teas by combining various herbs, such as:

Lemon balm with mint

Basil with mint, chamomile, orange peel and cinnamon

Chamomile with rose petals, jasmine and calendula

Lavender with mint, rosemary and cloves

Sage with thyme, marjoram, oregano and chamomile

Basil with chamomile, dittany, marjoram, wild mint, ironwort and cinnamon

✎ Infusion with chamomile, lemon verbena and mallow

1 teaspoon dried chamomile
1 teaspoon dried lemon verbena
1 teaspoon dried mallow petals
3 cups boiling water
sugar or honey

Rinse a teapot with hot water and put the herbs into it. Add boiling water, cover and steep for 5 minutes. Strain into cups and serve immediately with a little sugar or honey.

☞ Infusion with rose petals

1 cup boiling water
1/3 cup rose petals
honey or sugar to taste

It is prepared as above.

☞ Mint tea

3 cups water
3 tbsp fresh mint leaves
1 cinnamon stick
2 cloves

Boil water with cinnamon and cloves for 2 minutes. Remove from heat, put in mint leaves and let steep for 5 minutes. Strain and serve.

☞ Sage tea

1 tbsp dried sage
3 cups water

Put water in a kettle and bring to the boil. Add sage chopped in small pieces and boil for 3-4 more minutes. Filter and serve, preferably with honey.

☞ Victoria's tea

A tasty and aromatic tea, from herbs and fruit, inspired by Mrs Victoria Athanasiadou, from Chania, Crete.

2 apples
2 kiwis
3 tbsp mixed herbs (marjoram, linden, chamomile, dittany, mallow)
1 cinnamon stick
honey

Wash apples and cut in quarters. Peel kiwis and cut in quarters, too. Put in a casserole, cover with 5 cups water and boil until soft. Mash, strain through a clean cloth and put the juice in the casserole again. Add the herbs and boil for another 2 minutes. Strain and serve immediately with honey.

Cooking with herbs

Herbs are usually added to foods at the time of cooking. Nevertheless, there are other ways to include herbs in dishes. For example, you can use scented olive oil, butter or vinegar, flavoured sauces, flour, cheese or salt, even flavoured sugar for sweet preparations.

Raw salads, boiled or grilled meat, fish as well as vegetables can gain taste and flavour if they are served with olive oil or vinegar scented with herbs. Even the common sandwich tastes quite different if drizzled with scented olive oil or butter. You can also prepare different flavoured sauces in advance and have them available for use with various dishes. Cheese flavoured with herbs doesn't only taste better but can also be kept for longer. Flour flavoured with herbs imparts aroma to pastry or dough for pies or sweets. Flavoured sugar gives additional aroma to tea, milk, fruit juices, fruit salads, custards and sweets.

Harmony of taste and flavour

Food taste can be improved with the addition of the right herb seasoning. The art of creating flavour is usually a matter of personal preference. Sight, smell, taste, feeling and experience should guide you to find the right quantities of herbs, as well as the right herbs that go with each dish. Here are a few suggestions:

♦ **Oregano**: with vegetables, sauces, soups, meat, fish, poultry, pulses, pastas

♦ **Thyme**: with soups, stews, grilled, sauces, salads, pies, bread

♦ **Savory**: with soups, salads, pulses, meat, cheese, bread, fruit salads

♦ **Dill**: with soups, salads, sauces, minced meat, poultry, fish, pickles, cheese, omelets, pulses, pies, bread

♦ **Anise**: with eggs, cheese, fruits, meat, fish, salads, bread, biscuits, beverages

♦ **Bay leaves**: with soups, grilled or stewed meat and fish, chickpeas, lentils, custards, fruit salads

♦ **Basil**: with vegetables, soups, salads, eggs, seafood, meat, game, meatballs, pastas, bread, fruit

♦ **Tarragon**: with fish, salads, poultry, lamb, eggs, vinegar

♦ **Sage**: with stuffing, poultry and pork, pastas, pulses, bread, beverages, teas

♦ **Rosemary**: with meat, poultry, fish, seafood, omelets, soups, vegetables, fruit salads, savore sauce, bread

♦ **Mint**: with soups, sauces, salads, vegetables, pastas, pies, cheese, fruit, custards, beverages, teas

♦ **Coriander**: cilantro with sauces, salads, omelets, soups. Coriander seeds with stews, soups, sausage, pickles, custards, cheese salads, bread, biscuits

♦ **Lavender**: with salads, meat, cheese, fruit, sweets

♦ **Lemon verbena**: with soups, salads, meat, fish, fruit, sweets, beverages

♦ **Parsley**: with... anything! Meat, fish, soups, sauces, salads, omelets, pulses

♦ **Marjoram**: with stews, meat, fish, omelets, pastas, green pies, sausages, bread, beverages

♦ **Fennel**: with seafood, fish, snails, meat, soups, omelets, cheese, pastas, pulses, bread

♦ **Lemon balm**: with meat, poultry, fish, soups, cheese, fruit, beverages, teas

♦ **Celery**: with meat, fish, soups, salads, appetizers

♦ **Saffron**: with rice, risotto, buillabaisse, pastas, cheese, chicken, custards, bread, biscuits, sweets

HERB COMBINATIONS

Herbs can be combined to create successful mixtures, such as:

◆ **Fennel, parsley and lemon zest**
   (for fish)
◆ **Sage, chives, oregano and parsley**
   (for poultry)
◆ **Savory, marjoram and parsley**
   (for pulses)
◆ **Aniseed and orange zest**
   (for pork)
◆ **Basil, oregano and thyme**
   (for fish, poultry, rice and pastas)
◆ **Thyme, basil and parsley**
   (for bread and seafood)
◆ **Rosemary, chives, parsley and garlic**
   (for potatoes, beef, chicken)
◆ **Mint, garlic and parsley**
   (for lamb, seafood, vegetables)
◆ **Rosemary, thyme, savory, oregano, marjoram and garlic**
   (for grilled meats)
◆ **Calendula petals and chives**
   (for rice or chicken)
◆ **Basil, parsley, marjoram, rosemary, thyme and onion**
   (for boiled vegetables)
◆ **Oregano, basil, fennel seeds, dill and onion**
   (for fish and poultry)

There are traditional herb mixtures, such as "**bouquet garni**", which is a bunch consisting of equal amounts of bay leaves, thyme, parsley and rosemary. It is used in soups and stewed meat and fish.

Likewise, there is the mixture of "**herbes de Provence**", consisting of savory, thyme, lavender, rosemary, oregano and sage. You can use parsley and basil instead of oregano and sage. However, be sure to include the lavender buds. It is especially good with poultry and lamb, but also with rice, pastas, soups, potatoes, vegetables, fish, even with bread.

There is also the traditional French herb mix of «**fines herbes**», which is made up of equal parts of parsley, chervil, chives and tarragon.

This mix is perfectly suited for egg preparations, but also for vegetable soups, rice pilaf, potatoes, pastas and fish.

☞ **But, remember:** use them sparingly unless you are familiar with them. Begin by adding a small quantity until you have the right results.

Dried herbs have stronger fragrance; substitute one part of dried herbs for 3 parts of fresh ones.

The flavour of dried herbs becomes stronger the longer they are cooked, which is not the case with fresh herbs which should be added late in the cooking process (e.g. basil, chives, dill) or should be better added to foods just before serving.

However, herbs with a subtle flavour, such as parsley, release a stronger flavour with long, slow cooking.

OLIVE OIL SCENTED WITH HERBS

At least from the second millennium B.C. people used to flavour olive oil with herbs and prepare perfumes. In all probability, they used olive oil in cooking to improve taste. After 1450 B.C. knowledge about flavoured olive oil in the ancient world became more specific.

On Crete and in the Mycenaean centres of the Peloponnese, Mainland Greece and other regions, olive oil was flavoured with rose, sage and aromatic cyperus, according to evidence from clay Linear B tablets, the most ancient form of the Greek language.

In ancient Greece it was believed that it was olive oil that maintained the aroma of herbs. In Byzantium, olive oil was flavoured so that its quality was improved, just as was done on Crete until very recently.

Today we are aware of aromatic oils which the Byzantines made with dill, bay leaves, coriander and iris.

Greek popular medicine often used olive oil flavoured with the red petals of the poppy, with balsam (St John's wort), Spanish broom or other herbs. It was mainly intended for external use.

☙ HOW TO MAKE
SCENTED OLIVE OIL

Scented olive oil has currently a significant place in Mediterranean cooking, where it is used either in its raw state or cooked in food.

It gives aroma and taste to raw and boiled salads, meat, fish, even to sweets and pastry.

It can substitute butter at the beginning of a meal at the table, offering a natural taste in addition to being much more wholesome! You can have different scented olive oils to combine with the various dishes.

It is very easy to scent your own olive oil. The olive oil to be used should be of low acidity (0.1-0.9) and of a mild taste and aroma, so that it can elevate the scent of the herbs.

The herbs can be either fresh or dried or in the form of seeds. Fresh herbs should first be washed and dried completely.

The bottles used for storage should be sterilized. For this reason they are boiled in water for 5 minutes and left to dry.

They are usually made of transparent glass so that the herbs inside are visible, although it is advisable to use opaque bottles made of glass or clay, because sunlight affects the quality of olive oil and destroys its valuable antioxidative substances.

Even if you use a transparent bottle, it should be kept in a dark place. For longer periods of preservation, filter the olive oil and discard the herbs.

A range of aromatic plants can be used in different combinations depending on personal taste. A basic rule is to achieve a balance of tastes and aromas.

You can experiment although below, there are a few suggestions.

In general, you can place the herbs of your choice in a bottle, mixed with the olive oil and wait for 2-3 weeks.

Select a bottle which will allow you to remove the herbs later so that the olive oil can be preserved for longer.

♦ Olive oil can be flavoured with:

rosemary, bay laurel, fennel, spearmint, basil, dill, cedar, myrtle, thyme, oregano, Cretan dittany, marjoram, sage, coriander, tarragon and other herbs.

3-4 sprigs of herbs are required for every 2 cups of olive oil. Different aromatic plants can also be combined, such as:

- ♦ *oregano with thyme and garlic*
- ♦ *saffron or calendula with garlic*
- ♦ *basil with garlic*
- ♦ *tarragon with chervil*
- ♦ *cardamom with coriander*
- ♦ *aniseeds with cinnamon and clove*
- ♦ *dill with garlic*
- ♦ *thyme with lemon balm*
- ♦ *sun-dried tomatoes with basil or oregano*
- ♦ *rosemary with bay leaves*
- ♦ *poppy petals with cinnamon, clove and nutmeg*

⮞ Olive oil flavoured with fennel seeds

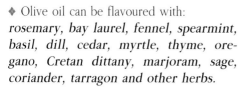

½ cup fennel seeds
3 cups olive oil

Heat fennel seeds until they release their aroma, then grind them in a food grinder. Transfer into a clean jar and fill with the olive oil.
Leave it in a dark place for a week, then strain out the seeds. Store the oil in a dark, cool place. Use in cooking, in raw salads or in bread making.

⮞ Olive oil flavoured with basil, thyme, rosemary and oregano

1 liter olive oil
1 tbsp basil
1 tbsp thyme
1 tbsp rosemary
1 tbsp oregano

Heat ½ cup olive oil, add the herbs and heat for 2-3 minutes.
Let the oil and herb mixture cool down, then strain and put in a bottle together with the rest of the olive oil. Cover and keep in a dark and cool place.
You can also put the herbs in the bottle, fill with the olive oil, then cover tightly and store in a dark, cool place. In this case it is ready for use after 2 weeks.

⮞ Herbs in olive oil

You can make scented olive oil and use it immediately, if you just put a considerable amount of chopped fresh herb (dill, parsley, basil etc) in a bowl filled with olive oil.
The oil is consumed together with the herb.

HERBAL BUTTER

Butter, like olive oil, can be scented with herbs and replace regular, non scented butter, giving, however, more flavour to the foods.

It can be used on sandwiches or on slices of bread with honey or marmalade, although it is advisable to use olive oil, as it is healthier. Making herbal butter is simple:

First allow butter, salted or unsalted, to come to room temperature. This can be done by heating the butter, together with the herbs, for a very short time.

Second, using a fork, blend in 1 tbsp lemon juice and 3 tbsp of any herb or combination of your favourite herbs. You can also use a little grated lemon zest.

Herbs suited for herbal butters are **cilantro, parsley, basil, dill, tarragon, mint, chives, scented-leaved pelargonium, marjoram, lavender, sage, lemon balm, thyme, oregano, cardamom and others.**

Third, place the herbal butter into a mould or roll into a log by wrapping it with waxed paper or plastic wrap.

Finally return to the refrigerator for 2-3 hours. Before serving, unwrap and cut in slices.

VINEGAR SCENTED WITH HERBS

Vinegar can be scented the same way as olive oil. It maintains the scent of the herbs and adds taste to the dishes. It is ideal for pickles. You can blend three parts of olive oil with one part of scented vinegar and make an excellent dressing for salads and sauces.

Almost any herb can be used for flavouring vinegar: oregano, thyme, marjoram, tarragon, mint, basil, rosemary, fennel, dill, lavender, coriander, caraway, chives and other herbs.

The herbs can be either dry or fresh or in the form of seeds. Fresh herbs should be clean and dry.

For ½ liter vinegar from white wine, use 4-5 sprigs of herbs. Place the herbs in a bottle and fill with the vinegar. Tap the bottle and wait for 10-15 days. Filter through a clean cloth and store in a cool, dark place.

Below are a few herb combinations for flavouring vinegar:

* *sage with parsley*
* *cilantro with garlic*
* *borage with dill*
* *spearmint with cardamom*
* *oregano with garlic*
* *rosemary with garlic*
* *fennel with parsley*
* *basil with garlic and bay laurel*
* *thyme with marjoram,*
  fresh oregano and rocket

⌇ Vinegar flavoured with myrtle

1 liter vinegar from wine
3-4 sprigs of myrtle

Rinse myrtle sprigs and pat dry. Put in a bottle and fill with the vinegar. Close tightly and wait for 10-15 days. Filter through a clean cloth and store in a glass bottle.

⌇ Vinegar flavoured with tarragon and bay leaves

½ cup tarragon
3 bay leaves

4-5 cloves
1 liter vinegar from wine

Proceed as above.

Vinegar flavoured with chives blossoms and savory

2 cups vinegar from white wine
5-6 chives blossoms
2 sprigs of savory or oregano

Put the herbs in a bottle, fill with the vinegar and leave in a dark place for 10 days. Filter through a clean cloth and store again in a dark, cool place. If desired, mix with a little honey and use over fish or vegetables.

Vinegar flavoured with herb blossoms

In the same way as above you can flavour vinegar with blossoms of **marjoram, nasturtium, oregano, dill, lavender, elder** or **borage**.

Rose-scented vinegar

It is the "oxyrothinon" of the ancient Greeks (Athenaeus, Deipn. 67f,) which is still made in many regions in Greece.

1 liter vinegar from wine
1,5 cup petals from aromatic roses

Wash and dry the rose petals. Put them in a bottle and fill with vinegar. Place the bottle in the sun and wait for 1 month. Stir often. Filter through a white cloth and store in bottles in a cool and dark place.

It can flavour salads which can be garnished with rose petals.

WINE SCENTED WITH HERBS

Dioscurides (1st c. A.D.) left us with detailed accounts about flavoured wine in antiquity. It was believed to be therapeutic and was used as a medicine against a great number of diseases. The ancients made wine with fruit (quinces, apples, pears, maple fruits, pomegranates, dates and other fruits). In addition to its medicinal qualities, it met the taste requirements of people at that time.

Wine was scented with myrtle fruits or leaves, lentisk, terebinth, pine resin ("rhetinitis"), pine nuts, cedar fruits, cypress, lavender, oregano, dittany, thyme, savory, wild mint, sage, dill ("anethinos"), aniseeds ("anisitis"), celery, fennel, parsley ("petroselinitis"), roses and other herbs.

Myrtle wine ("myrtinitis"), for example, was a remedy for rashes, gingivitis, tonsillitis, the treatment of dandruff and other complaints. It was prepared as follows:

They pounded myrtle leaves and fruits together and put about 4 kilos of crashed myrtle in about 10 liters of grape juice (must). Then they boiled the mixture until reduced to 8,5 liters...

Dittany wine was prepared like this: They enclosed about 16 grams of dittany in a clean cloth, dipped it in about 2 liters of must (grape juice) and left it there for 20 days. In a few regions on Crete, dittany wine is made even today in exactly the same way, only they use a smaller amount of dittany.

Just a few sprigs of dittany (according to Emm. Stratakis who prepares it) are enough to give a very pleasant smell to a barrel of wine! In antiquity, however, those wines were not made for taste but for medicinal purposes.

☞ **ATTENTION:** Today, there are very high quality wines and it is probably an exaggeration to flavour it.

Moreover, it is an advantage for the wine to maintain its natural characteristics, taste and aroma.

☙ Vermouth wine

The well known vermouth wine is made with herbs left in 15° wine, either white or red, for a period of time. Since wines are usually 11-12°, 40 ml of pure alcohol should be added. Sugar is added at the end to give a sweet taste.

The mixture of herbs to be used consists of dittany, oregano, cinnamon, thyme, hyssop, coriander, lemon peel, wild mint, chamomile, sage and rose petals. Twenty grams of herbs suffice for 1 liter of vermouth.

Put the herbs in the wine and leave them for about one month, shaking occasionally. Then filter and add half to one cup of sugar, according to your preference.

☙ Wine cocktail with scented-leaved pelargonium and sage

1 liter white wine
½ cup scented-leaved pelargonium syrup*
3-4 sage leaves or other herb (optional)
1 lemon and 1 orange, washed, dried and cut in slices

Mix all ingredients in a bowl and wait for a few hours. Serve with ice cubes.

* *scented-leaved pelargonium syrup, like other syrups, is made by boiling ½ cup pelargonium and 3/4 cup sugar in ½ cup water for 5-10 minutes. Finally the pelargonium is removed and discarded.*

HERB LIQUEURS

∾ Myrtle liqueur

1 liter raki
70 grams myrtle fruits
1 cup sugar
1 cup water

Place myrtle fruits in a container. Fill with raki and wait for one month.
Boil sugar with water for 5-6 minutes and let the syrup cool down. Filter the myrtle and raki mixture and stir in the syrup. Transfer the liqueur into clean bottles and keep in a cool, dark place.

∾ Scented-leaved pelargonium liqueur

100 grams scented-leaved pelargonium (both leaves and flowers)
3 cups sugar
2 liters water
1 liter raki

Wash and dry scented-leaved pelargonium. Prepare the syrup with the sugar and the water. Add pelargonium and boil for another 5-10 minutes. Turn off the heat and leave the pelargonium in the syrup for 2-3 days. Filter and share the syrup in 2-3 bottles.
Fill with the raki and store.

∾ Aniseed liqueur

1 liter raki
150 grams coarsely ground aniseeds
peel of 1 lemon or orange
2 cinnamon sticks, 10 cloves
600 grams sugar, 1,5 cup water

Put aniseeds, peel, cinnamon and cloves in an airtight container, fill with the raki and wait for at least one month. Open and add the syrup which you make by boiling the sugar with the water for 5 minutes. Stir and

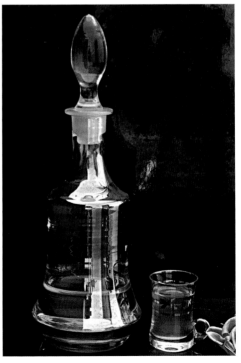

wait again for 10 days. Filter and store in bottles in a dark place.

✐ Rose petal liqueur

250 grams rose petals
1 kilo sugar
3 cups water
1 liter brandy
2 cinnamon sticks

Place rose petals, brandy and cinnamon in an airtight container and leave in the sun for one month. Boil sugar with water to make a thick syrup. Strain the brandy mixture through a clean cloth and blend with the syrup. Store the liqueur in airtight bottles and keep in a dark, cool place.

✐ Spearmint or peppermint liqueur

As above.

SALT FLAVOURED WITH HERBS

Salt can be flavoured with herbs of your preference. In this way not only can cooked food or salads be flavoured, but also the **required amount of salt added to the food can be reduced**. There are also suggestions to substitute salt in food with herbs, especially for people who have to exclude salt from their diet. Special herb mixtures can season food so that it doesn't taste saltless. You can use grain sea salt and dried herbs (parsley, basil, rosemary, thyme, savory, marjoram, ginger, lemon peel and others) in the desired combination. Grind the salt with the herbs of your preference (1 tbsp of herbs for each tbsp of salt) and store in airtight jars. Keep in a cool, dark place. Stir from time to time.

SUGAR FLAVOURED WITH HERBS

You can substitute or reduce the amount of sugar to be used in confectionery by using the following herbs: lemon balm, lemon verbena, lavender, scented-leaved pelargonium, spearmint, peppermint, rosemary, rose petals, hyssop, angelica. They can be ground all together or only the herbs that you like or have.

Scented sugar is a very good way to flavour your sweets or your beverages. Wash and dry herbs thoroughly.

Place in a jar alternating with sugar, taking care to leave a little space on top so that you can stir up the mixture from time to time.

Seal the jar and keep in a cool, dark place for 10 days. Don't forget to stir occasionally.

Before using the sugar, either remove the herbs or grind them in the mixer with the sugar.

You can add extra sugar every time you remove some of it.

CHEESE FLAVOURED WITH HERBS

The "green cheese", today's "farmer's cheese", was a peasant cheese made during medieval times.

To prepare it, certain herbs (mostly nettle) were added to milk to make it curdle. This was called "running the milk into curdles". After a large curd was made, it was pressed by weights to drain out the liquid.

Herbs were added to cheese for more than just curdling. Parsley and sage were added to soft cheeses to give not only the green colour but also flavour. Saffron and calendula were added for the yellow or orange colour and a different flavour.

Besides, herbs were used for their properties as conservatives.

⌇ Cheese with herbs

1 cup finely chopped fresh herbs
according to preference
(basil, oregano, marjoram, tarragon, parsley)
1 liter milk from sheep
or goat
1 lemon, a little salt

Put the pot with the milk and herbs on heat and bring to the boil.

Remove from fire and pour in the juice of the lemon stirring constantly until it curdles. Put in thick cheesecloth and allow it to strain.

Season with salt and place the cheese in the special container to strain better or consume it immediately.

⌇ Cheese in flavoured olive oil

1 kilo goat cheese
(or feta cheese)
3 tbsp dried thyme
3 tbsp dried rosemary
2 bay leaves
1-2 hot peppers or 1 tbsp peppercorns
5-6 coriander seeds
2 cloves of garlic (optional)
olive oil

Cut cheese into cubes and place in jars together with the herbs. Fill with olive oil and seal the jars. In 1-2 weeks it is ready for use.

⌇ Myzithra cheese balls

250 grams myzithra cheese
(fresh, soft cheese)
1 tbsp thyme or marjoram
or other herb, a little pepper
1 egg, 2-3 tbsp milk

1 cup crumbled toasted bread or chopped almonds
olive oil for frying

Combine myzithra cheese with the herb and the pepper and shape into balls as large as a walnut. Dip first in egg beaten with milk, then in bread crumbs, again in beaten egg, finally in bread-crumbs or almonds and fry in olive oil until golden brown.

*Cheese
in flavoured olive oil*

⸜ Yoghurt dressing with herbs (for vegetables)

1 cup yoghurt
1 cup bread crumbs
4 tbsp olive oil
1 tbsp lemon juice
1 clove mashed garlic
½ cup finely chopped parsley
1 tbsp finely chopped basil
1 tbsp finely chopped fresh oregano
½ cup chopped walnuts (optional)

Combine all ingredients well to make a thick sauce. Finally add walnuts.

⸜ Fried cheese ("saganaki") with herbs

150 grams fresh, soft cheese
150 grams feta cheese
1 tbsp finely chopped parsley
1 tbsp finely chopped chives
pepper to taste
1 cup ground toasted bread
and ground sesame seeds
olive oil for frying

Combine all ingredients well and make a cylinder. Refrigerate for 1-2 hours or longer. Heat very little olive oil in a frying pan. Cut rounds of cheese mixture, coat with bread and sesame and fry until lightly brown on both sides.
Place on absorbing paper for 1 minute and then serve.

Fried cheese with herbs

⸜ Cheese dip with walnuts or almonds and herbs

150 grams feta cheese
150 grams myzithra (ricotta or manouri)
150 grams grated cheese
(kefalotyri, parmesan or gruyere)
1 mashed clove of garlic or 1 tbsp finely chopped chives
2 tbsp finely chopped dill
2 tbsp finelly chopped spearmint
1 tbsp finelly chopped marjoram
2 tbsp olive oil
2 tbsp lemon juice
½ teaspoon pepper
½ cup chopped walnuts or almonds

Put feta, myzithra and grated cheese in a food processor. While it is working, add herbs, olive oil, lemon juice and pepper. Switch off the food processor and combine with walnuts or almonds. Transfer into a salad bowl and garnish with herb leaves and walnuts or almonds. Keep in the refrigerator for a few days. Flavours increase when left to stand. Serve on bread or rusks.

◆ *If desired, you can use a mixture of herbs, each in a small amount. You can choose among oregano, thyme, tarragon, anise, parsley, nasturtium, peppermint, fresh rosemary, marjoram, fennel or lemon balm.*
You can also put the cheese dip in the refrigerator for 1 hour and then form it into a log roll and sprinkle with sesame and poppy seeds. In this case, cut individual round servings.

⌇ Nasturtium flowers or tomatoes stuffed with cheese

You can prepare the above cheese dip and serve it inside cappuccino flowers or tomatoes, which you hollow first and sprinkle with a little salt.

You can also hollow **potatoes**, brush with a little olive oil, bake first in the oven and then stuff them with the dip.

⌇ Cheese spread with sun-dried tomatoes and herbs

2 cups soft goat's cheese
1 cup sun dried tomatoes in olive oil
1 tbsp fresh finely chopped oregano
2 tbsp finely chopped basil
1 tbsp fresh finely chopped thyme

Put all ingredients in the food processor and mix until mushy. *(If the sun-dried tomatoes are not preserved in olive oil, soak them in water first for 10-15 minutes).*

⌇ Cheese dip with calendula petals

250 grams soft cheese (manouri, myzithra, ricota, cottage cheese or curd cheese)
½ cup grated carrot
5-6 crushed calendula petals
pepper to taste

Place cheese in a bowl and mash with a fork. Add the rest of the ingredients and combine well.

Cheese dip with walnuts or almonds and herbs

⌇ Green peppers stuffed with cheese, spearmint and dill

7-8 green peppers
400 grams soft cheese or feta cheese
3 tbsp finely chopped dill
3 tbsp finely chopped spearmint
2 eggs
4-5 tbsp olive oil
a little salt, pepper

Wash and hollow peppers. Sprinkle with salt and pepper.
In a bowl combine cheese with eggs, dill and spearmint. Stuff the green peppers with this mixture, place on oiled baking pan, drizzle with the olive oil and bake in moderate heat until the peppers are soft.

⌇ Baked small cheese balls with herbs

½ kilo fresh cheese from sheep or goat
1 cup aromatic plants, finely chopped (parsley, fennel, spearmint and chives. You can also choose just one herb)
little salt, pepper
2 eggs
½ cup semolina flour

Mash cheese with a fork, add beaten eggs, herbs, very little salt, pepper and the semolina flour. Combine well. Divide the mixture into 10 parts, shape into balls and place on oiled baking tin. Press to broaden a little and bake in moderate heat until golden brown, for approximately half an hour.

Small cheese pies with parsley and spearmint.

❦ Small cheese pies with parsley and spearmint

For the **pastry**:
½ kilo flour
1 cup warm water
1 package dried yeast
½ teaspoon salt
3 tbsp olive oil
For the **filling**:
1 cup crumbled
feta cheese
1 cup grated goat's cheese
1 egg
1 tbsp finely chopped parsley
1 tbsp finely chopped spearmint
(*You can choose herbs from among dill, fennel, sage, cilantro or chives*)

With the above ingredients prepare smooth and elastic dough. Combine the ingredients for the filling.

Divide the dough into 15 parts, roll out round pieces, put 1 tbsp filling on each and fold to enclose the filling. Brush with beaten egg, sprinkle with sesame seeds and bake until golden brown.

❦ Large cheese pie with fennel and spearmint

For the **dough**:
½ cup milk or yoghurt
6 tbsp olive oil
1 egg
½ teaspoon salt
3 cups flour
For the **filling**: 3 tbsp olive oil
3 tbsp flour
2 cups milk
3 eggs
½ teaspoon pepper
1 cup crumbled feta cheese
1 cup crumbled myzithra cheese

Baked feta cheese with marjoram

2 cups of assorted grated cheese
(gruyere, kefalotyri, kasseri or other
cheese)
½ cup finely chopped fennel
½ cup finely chopped spearmint

Prepare the dough with the above ingredients and let it rest.

Prepare the filling: In a pot heat olive oil, stir in flour, then the hot milk and continue stirring until the mixture thickens. Remove from heat and stir in the beaten eggs, pepper, cheese, fennel and spearmint.

Roll out the dough and layer it on the bottom and sides of an oiled baking tin. Spread the filling over it. Brush with a beaten egg and bake in moderate heat until golden brown.

You can choose from a range of herbs, such as dill, sage, cilantro, chives and others.

With the same dough and the same filling you can make tasty, flavoured small cheese pies: cut round pieces of dough, put 1 teaspoon of filling on each one, fold in two, brush with beaten egg and bake.

❧ Baked feta cheese with marjoram

100 grams feta cheese in one slice
1 medium grated tomato
½ teaspoon marjoram
little salt
pepper

Place the slice of feta on a piece of aluminum foil or grease-proof paper.

Sprinkle with the tomato, salt, pepper and marjoram, wrap and bake for 10 minutes. Serve while still hot.

HERB SAUCES
AND DRESSINGS

❧ Oil and vinegar or oil and lemon dressing flavoured with herbs

You can make your own sauces instead of buying them at the supermarket. To the classic oil and vinegar or oil and lemon dressing you can add the herbs of your preference. In addition to offering taste and flavour, it is healthy.

The ratio is 3 parts of olive oil to 1 part of vinegar or lemon juice. Add 1 teaspoon dried herbs or 1 tablespoon fresh herbs for ½ cup dressing. If using dried herbs, rub them with your fingers to release their aroma.

The herbs that can be used are: **oregano, parsley, spearmint, peppermint, rosemary, marjoram, savory, thyme, basil, tarragon, chives, dill, caraway, fennel, water cress, chervil, mustard seeds.**

You can combine different flavoured olive oils or vinegars for fast flavoured dressings. Olive oil and vinegar mostly dresses green salad while olive oil and lemon marries well with meat or fish, whether boiled or grilled.

❧ Spearmint sauce

4 tbsp fresh finely chopped spearmint
4 tbsp lemon juice or vinegar
4 tbsp olive oil
1 teaspoon sugar
1 clove of garlic (optional)
salt, pepper

Put all ingredients in a pot and cook until mushy.
Spearmint sauce accompanies boiled or grilled meat (principally lamb).

❧ Thyme sauce (for meat or fish)

1 cup bread crumbs
6 tbsp olive oil
2 tbsp vinegar
1 clove of garlic
1 tbsp thyme
salt, pepper

Place bread, olive oil, vinegar, garlic, salt, pepper and 4-5 tbsp water in a food processor and mash them. Stir in thyme and transfer into a sauce bowl.

❧ Sauce with anchovies and herbs, for pastas

5-6 tbsp olive oil
2 cloves of chopped garlic
5 chopped anchovies
½ kilo grated tomatoes
1 tbsp basil
1 teaspoon oregano
pepper

Heat olive oil in a pan and sauté garlic for a very short time so that it doesn't get brown. Add anchovies and stir for 5-6 minutes to mash them. Pour in tomatoes, herbs, pepper and a little water and simmer until the sauce thickens.

❧ Sauce with herbs and sun-dried tomatoes

2 tbsp dried basil
1 teaspoon thyme
2 cloves of garlic
pepper

1-2 tbsp capers (optional)
3 tbsp pine nuts or chopped walnuts
½ cup sun-dried tomatoes
together with their oil

Combine all ingredients in the mixer. Transfer in a bowl or jar and keep in the refrigerator for a few days.

✑ Pesto sauce

This is also a way of preserving herbs. It is used on spaghetti, bread, in cheese salads, in vegetable and other soups, in potato purée, potato salad, on grilled meat or fish.
It is commonly prepared with basil, but can also be made with marjoram, sage, cilantro, chervil, lemon balm, star-of-Bethlehem, tarragon, mint, chives, rocket or oregano.

✑ Basil pesto

1 cup fresh basil leaves
2 minced cloves of garlic
½ teaspoon salt, pepper
3 tbsp chopped walnuts
or pine nuts
½ cup olive oil
½ cup grated cheese
(kefalotyri or parmezan)

Wash and dry basil. Place in a mortar or food processor together with garlic, salt, pepper and walnuts or pine nuts.
Add olive oil, little by little, while the machine is running, until it is absorbed.
Combine with cheese and transfer to a bowl or store in jars with a little olive oil on top.

✑ Rocket pesto

As above, with the difference that basil is substituted with arugula (rocket).
3-4 tbsp basil leaves, parsley or cilantro are also added.

Rocket pesto.

✑ Pesto with sorrel and chives

1 cup sorrel
½ cup chives
½ cup parsley
5 tbsp pine nuts or walnuts
½ cup olive oil
salt, pepper

Proceed as above.

✑ Mayonnaise with herbs

1 cup olive oil
1 teaspoon powdered mustard
2 egg yolks
2 tbsp lemon juice or vinegar
salt, pepper
2 tbsp finely chopped herbs (parsley, chervil, tarragon)

(A number of herbs can be used, such as basil, thyme, dill, watercress, cilantro, mint, borage, sorrel)

Wash herbs, dry completely and grind in the electric mixer. Add yolks, mustard, salt and pepper.
Pour in olive oil, little by little, and finally lemon juice or vinegar, stirring continuously. It can be stored in an airtight jar for up to 3 months.

♦ *It accompanies mostly fish, both boiled and grilled.*

♦ *You can also flavour mayonnaise which is readily available in supermarkets.*

HERB SOUPS

≈ Soup with chestnuts

½ kilo veal or beef in cubes
½ kilo chestnuts
2 onions cut in four
2 cloves of garlic
1 finely chopped leek
2 finely chopped sprigs of celery
1 bunch of herbs (parsley, bay leaves, thyme)
peel of 1 orange
salt, pepper

Put meat in a pot with 2,5 liters water, salt and pepper. When it starts to boil remove the scum from the surface.
In another pot put water and the chestnuts and boil for 5 minutes. Peel them and add to the pot with the meat.

Add the onion, garlic, leek, celery, the bunch of herbs, the peel and a little pepper and simmer for about 2 hours. Remove meat, the bunch of herbs and the peel and mash the rest. Serve the soup immediately.
Variation: A few saffron stamens can be added.

≈ Tomato soup with basil or spearmint

A summer dish, particularly of the first fortnight of August.

3-4 tbsp olive oil
1 grated onion
1 kilo grated tomatoes
salt, pepper
1,5 liter water or stock
½ cup cracked wheat or

other type of pasta
1 tbsp finely chopped basil or spearmint
1 teaspoon thyme
2 bay leaves

Heat olive oil in a pot and sauté the onion until soft. Add tomatoes, salt and pepper and cook for 3 minutes.
Pour in water or stock, bay leaves and thyme

Sorrel soup in egg-lemon sauce

and simmer for another 10 minutes after it has come to the boil. Finally add the pasta and the basil and cook for another 20 minutes. Serve the soup garnished with basil or spearmint leaves.

◆ **Variation:** *You can serve tomato soup with 1 tbsp yoghurt on each dish. You can also use fresh oregano leaves.*

⬅ Soup with herbs

½ cup from each of the following: spinach, nasturtium, beet leaves, rocket, sorrel

2 sprigs from each of the following herbs: basil, fennel, spearmint, parsley, celery
3 spring onions
1 leek
2 carrots
2 liters water
5-6 tbsp olive oil
salt, 5-6 peppercorns
2-3 tbsp flour

Wash herbs and vegetables, chop them and cook in a pot with the water, olive oil, salt and pepper for at least 1 hour. Strain through a sieve pressing a little with your fingers and return to the pot. Dilute flour in a little water, pour the mixture into the pot and boil for 5-10 more minutes.
Serve the soup garnished with spearmint or basil leaves.

⬅ Sorrel soup in egg-lemon sauce

3 finely chopped spring onions
2 tbsp finely chopped chives
3 tbsp olive oil
2 potatoes cut into dice
2 cups finely chopped sorrel
salt, pepper
2 eggs, 2 lemons
1,5 liter water or vegetable broth

In a large saucepan heat olive oil and sauté onion, chives and potatoes for 5 minutes. Add sorrel, water or vegetable broth, salt and pepper and continue to boil for another 15-20 minutes.
Switch off the heat and prepare the egg-lemon sauce: Beat egg whites and continue with yolks, lemon juice and a little broth from the saucepan so that the temperature is balanced.
Remove the pan from the heat and stir egg-lemon sauce into it.

⮞ Soup with asparagus and Venus' combs

½ kilo asparagus
2 cups milk
1 finely chopped onion
3 tbsp olive oil or butter
1 cup finely chopped Venus' combs

⮞ Soup with pumpkin

1 kilo pumpkin cut in quarters
2 finely chopped onions
2 finely chopped cloves of garlic (chives or leeks)
3-4 tbsp olive oil
2 potatoes cut in quarters

Soup with pumpkin

2 tbsp flour
salt, pepper

Wash and clean asparagus and Venus' combs and boil them in the milk for 5-6 minutes. Mash in the electric mixer together with the milk until creamy.
Heat olive oil in a pot and sauté onion for 2-3 minutes. Stir in flour and then the creamy herb mixture.
Pour in 2 cups hot water, salt and pepper and bring to the boil. Turn off the heat and serve the soup.

1 bunch of herbs
(parsley, basil, thyme, sage)
2 liters water
salt, pepper
1 cup strained yoghurt
or grated cheese

In a large saucepan heat olive oil and sauté onion and garlic or leeks for 2-3 minutes. Add pumpkin, potatoes, herbs and water and simmer until pumpkin is soft.
Remove herbs and mash the rest.
Season with salt and pepper.

Serve with 1 tbsp yoghurt or grated cheese on each dish and garnish with a basil leaf.

♦ **Variation**: *Add ½ kilo finely chopped tomatoes.*

∽ Chicken soup with herbs in egg-lemon sauce

1 chicken cut in pieces
½ cup finely chopped fennel
1 tbsp ground fennel seeds
1 coarsely chopped onion
½ cup leeks in rounds
½ cup finely chopped celery
½ cup finely chopped parsley
2 bay leaves
3-4 sage leaves
1 tbsp thyme
1 chopped green pepper
½ cup rice
salt, pepper
2 eggs, 2 lemons

Place chicken and 2 liters water in a large pot. When it starts boiling, remove the scum from the surface. Add the rest of the in-gredients, except for the rice, and simmer until chicken is soft, about 1 hour.
Take the chicken and bay leaves out of the pot and stir in the rice, salt and pepper.
Boil for 10 minutes until rice is ready and prepare the egg-lemon sauce:
Beat egg-whites and

continue with yolks, lemon juice and a little broth from the pot so that the temperature is balanced. Remove the pot from the heat and stir egg-lemon sauce into it.

∽ Meat soup with herbs

1 kilo meat
1-2 onions
2 garlic cloves
1 bunch of herbs
(celery, bay leaves, thyme, mint, parsley)
3 carrots and 2 potatoes
2 tomatoes
4-5 cloves
2-3 tbsp olive oil
salt, pepper

Wash meat, cut into pieces and put in a large pot with 2,5 liters water and a little salt. Turn on heat and remove the scum from the surface as it's coming to the boil. Add onions, cloves, garlic and the bunch of herbs and boil for about 50 minutes.
Then add carrots, potatoes, salt and pepper and boil for another 50 minutes. Take the meat and the vegetables out of the pot and put aside. Remove herbs, too, and serve the soup immediately. Meat and vegetables are served on separate platters.
(You can also add some rice or cracked wheat).

APPETIZERS - HERB SALADS

✑ Eggplant dip with herbs

You can use one or more herbs according to taste (basil, oregano, marjoram, thyme, cilantro, parsley, anise, mint, ginger).

1 kilo large eggplants
2-3 mashed garlic cloves
1 tbsp marjoram or any of the above herbs
salt, pepper
2-3 tbsp lemon juice, vinegar or juice of unripe grapes
½ cup olive oil

Wash eggplants and roast either in the oven or on heat until soft.
As soon as they cool down a little, peel and mash them in the mixer. Add garlic, salt, pepper, lemon juice and olive oil a little at a time and combine well.
Mix in the herb of your preference and transfer the dip to a salad bowl.

◆ **Variation:** Roast garlic (unpeeled) in the oven together with the eggplants and then peel, mash, and add to the dip.

✑ Eggplant dip with sun-dried tomatoes and basil

As above. In the end add ½ cup sun-dried tomatoes and 2 tbsp finely chopped basil.

✑ Eggplant salad with pomegranate juice

1 kilo large eggplants
½ kilo finely chopped tomatoes
½ cup juice of unripe grapes
1 cup of pomegranate juice
2 onions
1 teaspoon marjoram
1 teaspoon mint
    salt, pepper

Wash eggplants and roast them in the oven for half an hour.
When they have cooled down a little, peel and finely chop them.
Put in a casserole, drizzle with the juices, add salt and pepper and simmer for 10 minutes. Grate onion and add it to the pot together with the marjoram and mint.
Turn off heat and add tomatoes. Stir and serve.

✑ Pickled bulbs of tassel hyacinth

1 kilo bulbs
2 cups vinegar
1,5 tbsp salt

Peel the bulbs of tassel hyacinth, rinse well and boil in ample water for 15 minutes. Discard water and repeat twice.
After the third time, strain and dry them.

Pickled bulbs of tassel hyacinth.

Picked capers (leaves, sprigs and buds).

Place in a jar with the salt and vinegar. Cover with a thin layer of olive oil, seal the jar and store in a cool, dark place.

Serve with olive oil and finely chopped fresh garlic leaves or dill.

➤ Pickled shallots with mint

As above. You can add 2 tbsp of dried mint to the jar with the shallots.

➤ Pickled caper or nasturtium buds

½ kilo fresh caper or nasturtium buds
2 cups vinegar
1 tbsp salt
3-4 peppercorns
½ cup olive oil

Wash capers 2-3 times and boil in salted water for 5 minutes.

Drain on a clean towel. Place in glass jars with salt, pepper and vinegar to cover them. On top, pour a thin layer of olive oil, seal the jar and keep in a cool, dark place.

◆ *Nasturtium buds are harvested after the flowers have fallen.*

➤ Broad beans in olive oil with fennel

½ kilo seeds from fresh broad beans
1 tbsp salt
the juice of 4 lemons
olive oil
2-3 sprigs of fennel

Boil broad beans in 1 liter of water, adding salt and the juice of 1 lemon. Drain well. Place in a glass jar and cover with the lemon juice and olive oil.

Add fennel sprigs and close the jar. Store in a dark, cool place.

↪ Salad with broad beans and fennel

½ kilo fresh broad beans
1 bunch fennel tops
1 bunch wild carrots
1-2 garlic leaves or chives
salt, olive oil

Boil broad beans and herbs in salted water for 10-15 minutes. Strain and serve drizzled with olive oil and sprinkled with finely chopped garlic leaves or chives.

↪ Tomato slices with cheese and spearmint

100 grams goat's cheese,
feta or mozzarela
2 tomatoes
2 tbsp basil or spearmint leaves
pepper
3 tbsp olive oil (preferably flavoured olive oil)

Cut cheese into thin slices and each tomato into 4-6 horizontal slices. Arrange tomato slices on a plate, cover with the cheese slices, sprinkle with pepper and finely chopped spearmint or basil, drizzle with olive oil and serve.

↪ Rice salad with spearmint or dill

2 cups rice
½ kilo peas
1 finely chopped onion
2 tbsp finely chopped dill or spearmint
1 teaspoon grated ginger
1 teaspoon grated lemon rind
2 tbsp lemon juice
½ cup grated cheese
½ cup olive oil
salt, freshly ground pepper

Boil rice in 5 cups water until water is absorbed. Rinse and strain.
Heat olive oil in a pan and sauté onion for 5 minutes. Add peas and 1 cup water and cook until soft. Strain and mix with the rice and the rest of the ingredients.

↪ Almond dip with dill or sage

1 cup almonds, blanched, roasted and chopped
2 cups yoghurt
2 tbsp olive oil
1 tbsp lemon juice
salt, pepper

½ teaspoon crushed dried sage or
2 tbsp finely chopped fresh dill

Beat yoghurt with salt, pepper, sage or dill,
olive oil and lemon juice.
Add almonds and mix well. Garnish with
finely chopped dill or sage leaves.

Almond dip with dill or sage.

⌒ Salad with wild greens and herbs

3 cups wild greens (chicory, spine
chicory, dandelion, Venus' combs, rocket,
cress, smooth saw thistles)
½ cup finely chopped fresh onions
2 tbsp vinegar
6 tbsp olive oil
salt, pepper
3 tbsp chopped walnuts, sesame seeds
or pine nuts

Wash and chop the greens and place in
a salad bowl. Blend vinegar with olive
oil, salt and pepper, beating constantly with
the whisk. Toss the dressing over the greens
and sprinkle with the nuts.

⌒ Salad with spinach, rocket and sesame seeds

2 cups spinach
1 cup rocket
1 finely chopped spring onion
1 teaspoon salt
5 tbsp olive oil
2 tbsp lemon juice
2 tbsp sesame seeds

Wash and chop spinach and rocket and put
in a salad bowl together with the onion.
Whisk olive oil, lemon juice and salt until
well blended and toss to coat the salad.
Sprinkle with sesame seeds.

⌒ Salad with spinach, broccoli and poppy-seed dressing

As above. Substitute rocket with small
broccoli bouquets and the sesame seeds with
poppy seeds.

⌒ Salad with spinach, cheese and sesame seeds

As above. Add 5-6 scales of goat's cheese.

⌒ Salad with rocket, nasturtium and cheese

As above. Enrich the salad with 1 cup
nasturtium leaves and flowers.

⌒ Salad with spinach, yoghurt and borage

200 grams coarsely chopped spinach
1 spring onion, finely chopped
1 cup tender borage leaves,
 finely chopped

*Right: Salad with spinach,
rocket and sesame seeds.*

Salad with spinach, cheese and sesame seeds

Lettuce salad with lemon blossoms

2 tbsp finely chopped dill
1 tbsp finely chopped tarragon
1 tbsp finely chopped spearmint
5 tbsp olive oil
1 cup yoghurt
2 tbsp lemon juice or vinegar
1 mashed garlic clove
salt, pepper

Place all ingredients in a salad bowl. Beat yoghurt with olive oil, lemon juice or vinegar and garlic and pour the dressing over the salad.

⤙ Peasant salad with herb dressing

1 medium chopped lettuce
2 medium tomatoes cut into wedges
2 small cucumbers cut in rounds
1 onion cut in slices
½ cup olives
½ cup crumbled feta cheese
For the **dressing**: 5-6 tbsp olive oil
3 tbsp lemon juice
1 teaspoon thyme or oregano
1 tbsp finely chopped lemon balm
1 tbsp finely chopped basil
salt and pepper to taste

Place all ingredients in a salad bowl. In another bowl whisk all ingredients for the dressing and pour over the salad. Toss gently and serve.

⤙ Lettuce salad with lemon blossoms

1 lettuce
½ cup rocket
1 spring onion, finely chopped
1 grated apple (optional)
For the **dressing**: 5-6 tbsp olive oil
1 tbsp lemon juice
1 tbsp vinegar
1 tbsp honey

1 tbsp finely chopped dill
1 tbsp finely chopped parsley
salt, pepper
3-4 tender tops from lemon shoots
or lemon blossoms

Wash and chop spinach and rocket and place in a salad bowl together with the other ingredients. In another bowl whisk the ingredients for the dressing until well blended and pour over the salad. Toss, garnish with the lemon flowers and serve.

◆ *You can sprinkle with 2 tbsp pomegranate seeds and 2 tbsp coarsely chopped walnuts.*

➬ Salad with purslane and herbs

1 cup coarsely chopped purslane
2 finely chopped fresh onions
½ cup finely chopped parsley
4 tbsp finely chopped dill
2 tbsp finely chopped mint
2 tbsp finely chopped basil
1 finely chopped garlic clove or chives
½ cup crumbled feta cheese (optional)
salt, 5 tbsp olive oil
2 tbsp vinegar

Toss purslane, onion and herbs in a salad bowl. Whisk olive oil with salt, garlic and vinegar and pour over the salad. Toss well and let it stand for a while before it is served.

◆ *Tomato, lettuce, cucumber or green pepper can also be added. The salad can be served with crutons or pieces of "paximathi" (rusks), or grilled slices of bread.*

➬ Potato salad with artichokes and asparagus

2 boiled potatoes
3 hard-boiled eggs

1 spring onion, finely chopped
3-4 boiled artichoke hearts
250 grams boiled asparagus
½ cup finely chopped parsley
½ cup olive oil
3 tbsp lemon juice or vinegar
salt, pepper
1 tbsp oregano, thyme or marjoram

Wash potatoes and boil them together with the eggs for half an hour. Prepare the artichokes (remove the outer leaves, trim the

chokes and rub with lemon juice). Cut out the hard part from the asparagus and boil them together with the artichokes for 8-10 minutes until soft. Peel the potatoes and the eggs, cut in pieces and place in a salad bowl. Add asparagus and artichokes cut in slices. Whisk olive oil with salt, pepper, parsley, oregano, lemon juice or vinegar to blend well and drizzle over the salad.

Potato salad with nasturtium and cheese

To the above salad add ½ cup nasturtium leaves and flowers, 5-6 olives, 100 grams diced gruyere cheese and ½ cup chopped walnuts.

Shrimp salad with tarragon or lemon balm

1 medium lettuce
1 spring onion
½ kilo shrimps
salt, pepper
6 tbsp olive oil

the juice of 1 lemon or 2 tbsp vinegar
1 teaspoon tarragon or lemon balm

Wash and finely chop lettuce and spring onion and place in a salad bowl. Wash shrimps, boil them for 10 minutes, strain, peel and place on top of the greens. Whisk olive oil with lemon juice or vinegar, tarragon or lemon balm, salt and pepper and pour over the salad.

Salad with rock samphire and capers

2 cups rock samphire
2 tbsp fresh caper buds or 1 cup fresh leaves, sprigs and buds
4 tbsp olive oil
1 tbsp vinegar
½ cup olives

Boil rock samphire and capers and strain. Place in a salad bowl, sprinkle with salt, drizzle with olive oil and vinegar and garnish with olives.

Lentil salad with herbs

½ kilo lentils
1 onion cut into quarters
2 garlic cloves
1 bunch of herbs
(parsley, thyme, bay leaves)
salt, pepper
2 tbsp vinegar
5-6 tbsp olive oil

Put lentils in a pot, cover with water, boil for 10 minutes and strain. Return the lentils to the pot, cover again with water, add onion, garlic, thyme, parsley, bay leaves, salt and pepper. Boil for half an hour until lentils are cooked but not overcooked. Strain, remove the herbs and put lentils in a salad bowl. Whisk olive oil with vinegar, drizzle over the lentils and sprinkle with finely chopped parsley or fresh thyme.

Tabbouleh with parsley and spearmint

A Lebanese salad made with bulgur and herbs.

1 cup bulgur
1 cup hot water
3 spring onions, finely chopped
½ kilo tomatoes, cut in dice
2 cups finely chopped parsley
½ cup finely chopped spearmint
3 tbsp finely chopped lemon balm
salt, 5-6 tbsp olive oil
juice of 2 lemons

Moisten bulgur in water for one hour. Strain, place in a bowl and mix with the rest of the ingredients.
Serve in romaine lettuce leaves.

∽ Dry bean and wheat salad

1 cup dry beans
1 cup wheat
2-3 sprigs of savory
2 spring onions, finely chopped
½ cup finely chopped dill
salt, pepper
5 tbsp olive oil
2 tbsp lemon juice

Soak beans and wheat in water from the evening before. The following day strain and place in a pot with the savory. Cover with water and boil until soft. Strain and transfer to a salad bowl. Whisk olive oil with lemon juice, salt and pepper and pour over the salad. Sprinkle with finely chopped spring onion and dill.

∽ Salad with dry beans, wheat, chives and rocket

As above. Flavour the salad with rocket and chives.

OLIVES
FLAVOURED WITH HERBS

Edible olives can gain a unique taste and flavour with the addition of herbs. A range of herbs can be used for this, such as *fennel, dill, cumin, celery, lentisk seeds, bay leaves, thyme, oregano, rosemary, coriander, lemon peel etc.* Black olives are marinated in olive oil, vinegar and herbs, while green olives are marinated in olive oil, lemon juice and herbs.

∽ Olives with thyme and coriander

1 cup green olives
1 cup black olives
1 lemon in wedges
1 tbsp coriander seeds
2 cloves of garlic
1 sprig of thyme
1 hot pepper
olive oil

Place all ingredients in a jar and fill with olive oil. Store in a dark, cool place.

∽ Tapenade with thyme

2 cups pitted olives
1 garlic clove
the juice of 1 lemon
2-3 anchovies
1 tbsp thyme
pepper

Put anchovies in water for 10-15 minutes to remove salt. Put all ingredients in a mixer and stir until mushy.

∽ Tapenade with capers and chervil

As above. Instead of thyme, add 2 tbsp fresh parsley and 2 tbsp chervil, finely chopped, as well as 2 tbsp capers.

PASTAS

ꕔ Spaghetti with walnuts and basil

½ kilo pasta
(spaghetti or tagliatelle) boiled al dente
For the **sauce**:
3 tbsp olive oil
1 onion, finely chopped
1/3 cup white wine
1 clove garlic, finely chopped
½ kilo finely chopped tomatoes
4-5 sun-dried tomatoes
1 cup chopped walnuts
2 tbsp finely chopped basil
salt and pepper to taste

Heat olive oil in a pan and sauté onion until translucent.
Add garlic, wine, walnuts and tomatoes (both fresh and dried) and simmer for half an hour until the sauce thickens. Season with salt, pepper and basil and turn off the heat.
Serve spaghetti with the sauce and, optionally, sprinkle with grated cheese.

ꕔ Spaghetti with vegetables and herbs

To the above sauce add 1 eggplant and 2 courgettes, cut in dice.

ꕔ Pasta with tapenade

½ kilo pasta (spaghetti or tagliatelle)
For the **sauce:**
1 cup black olives
½ cup capers
3-4 anchovies (optional)
1 or ½ hot pepper without the seeds
½ cup parsley
½ cup sun-dried tomatoes
with a little from their oil
1 cup grated cheese

Prepare the tapenade: Put olives, capers, anchovies, hot pepper, parsley and sun-dried tomatoes in the mixer and stir until mushy.
Boil spaghetti or tagliatelle al dente. Strain and return to the pan. Pour tapenade over

*Spaghetti
with walnuts
and basil*

the pasta, stir and turn off heat.
Serve sprinkled with grated cheese and finely chopped parsley.

✐ Spaghetti with poppy seeds

½ kilo spaghetti No 7
4 tbsp olive oil
1 onion cut into wedges
3 garlic cloves
3 tbsp poppy seeds
salt
1 cup grated cheese (optional)
finely chopped dill or fennel

Boil spaghetti in ample salted water for 5-6 minutes, strain and mix with 2 tbsp olive oil. Heat remaining olive oil in a pan and sauté onion and garlic for 2-3 minutes.
Take them out and stir in poppy seeds.
Add spaghetti, stir a couple of times and turn off heat. Serve sprinkled with dill or fennel or, if desired, with cheese.

✐ Pasta with seafood and herbs

½ kilo spaghetti

For the sauce:
200 grams squid cut into thin strips
200 grams octopus in small pieces
300 grams shrimps
1 kilo shellfish (mussels, cockles, scallops)
5-6 tbsp olive oil
3 spring onions, finely chopped
½ cup finely chopped parsley
2 finely chopped garlic cloves
1 teaspoon basil
1 teaspoon oregano
1 kilo finely chopped tomatoes
½ cup white wine
salt, pepper

Prepare the **sauce**: Heat olive oil in a pan and sauté onion until translucent.
Add garlic, squid and octopus and cook for half an hour.
Then add shellfish and cook for a short time (5-6 minutes) in order for them to open (discard those that do not open).
Pour in tomato, season with basil, oregano, salt and pepper and cook until the sauce thickens.

*Spaghetti
with poppy seeds*

☞ Rice pilaf with herbs

2 cups rice
5 tbsp olive oil
1 grated onion
½ cup white wine
1 tbsp from each of the following herbs:
parsley, celery, dill, cilantro, thyme, marjoram, chives, chervil, water cress
salt and pepper to taste

Heat olive oil in a skillet and sauté onion until translucent. Add rice, herbs, salt and pepper and cook for a few minutes stirring 2-3 times. Pour in wine and then 5 cups water and stir. Cook until water is absorbed, 10-15 minutes, stirring often.

Remove skillet from the ring, cover with a clean towel and let the pilaf stand for 10 minutes before being served.

☞ Rice pilaf with vegetables and herbs

To the above pilaf add chopped vegetables of your preference, such as asparagus, carrots, artichokes, mushrooms. For the preparation proceed as above.

☞ Rice pilaf with saffron

2 cups rice
6 tbsp olive oil
½ cup coarsely chopped almonds
½ cup raisins
1 tbsp ground coriander seeds
1 teaspoon cumin or caraway
½ teaspoon saffron
salt, pepper

Soak raisins in water for 10-15 minutes and drain.

Heat olive oil in a pan and sauté almonds, coriander and cumin for 2-3 minutes. Add rice and stir a couple of times. Stir in raisins, saffron dissolved in a little water, 5 cups water, salt and pepper and cook for 10 minutes, stirring often. Turn off heat, cover with a clean towel for 10-15 minutes and serve.

☞ Cracked wheat with milk and spearmint

1 cup cracked wheat or bulgur
4 cups all-fat milk
1 tbsp finely chopped spearmint
salt, pepper

Simmer cracked wheat or bulgur in milk for 15 minutes after it has come to the boil, stirring continuously so that it doesn't stick to the bottom of the pan.

Finally add spearmint, salt and pepper and serve.

Rice pilaf with vegetables and herbs

VEGETABLES

Nettle pie with flavoured pastry dough

½ kilo tender nettles
½ kilo spinach
2 grated onions
4 tbsp olive oil
½ cup finely chopped spearmint
½ cup finely chopped fennel
salt, pepper
1 cup ground toasted bread

For the **pastry dough**:
½ cup water
½ cup milk
6 tbsp olive oil
1 teaspoon salt
1 teaspoon thyme or basil
½ kilo flour

Prepare the dough: Mix flour with salt and selected herb. Make a hole in the center and pour in the liquids. Combine, knead smooth and elastic dough and set aside.
Meanwhile boil nettle with spinach for 5 minutes, strain and chop.
Brown onion in olive oil, add spinach, nettles and fennel and sauté until water has evaporated. Turn off heat and stir in spearmint, salt, pepper and ground toasted bread.
Roll half the dough out and cover the bottom and the sides of an oiled baking pan.
Spread the greens over the phyllo sheet and cover with the other sheet which you make by rolling out the remaining half of the dough. Join the ends of the two layers of dough, brush the surface of the pie with beaten egg, sprinkle with sesame seeds and bake until golden brown.

Fennel pie

For the filling:
½ kilo fennel
1 cup finely chopped spring onions
250 grams feta cheese
250 grams fresh myzithra
or other cheese
5 eggs
3 tbsp olive oil
a little salt, pepper

For the phyllo dough and the preparation, proceed as above.

Baked spinach pilaf with herbs

1 kilo spinach
½ cup olive oil
1 finely chopped leeks
3 finely chopped spring onions
½ cup finely chopped fennel
½ cup finely chopped dill
½ cup finely chopped parsley
250 grams rice
salt, pepper
1 cup grated cheese

Heat olive oil in a pan and sauté onion, leek, fennel and dill.
Add rice, stir a couple of times and then pour in 2,5 cups water. Boil for a few minutes until rice is half done. In a separate pot boil spinach in water for 5 minutes, strain and add it to the pot with the rice. Stir and transfer the whole mixture into an oiled oven-proof pan. Sprinkle with the cheese and bake for about 20 minutes.

Spinach pilaf with nettles

To the above spinach pilaf add one cup tender nettles.

◡ Mallow pilaf

It is prepared like spinach pilaf, but cooking is completed in the casserole, not in the oven. Of course, mallow is used instead of spinach.

◡ Sautéed greens with mustard seeds

1 kilo mustard
5 tbsp olive oil
2 tbsp mustard seeds
1 finely chopped onion
salt, pepper

Boil greens in water for 5 minutes and strain. Heat olive oil in a pan and sauté onion and seeds for 5 minutes.
Add mustard, salt and pepper and cook until water has evaporated, stirring occasionally.

◡ Fresh broad beans with herbs in egg-lemon sauce

1 kilo fresh broad beans
½ cup olive oil
1 cup finely chopped fennel
1-2 garlic leaves, finely chopped
1 teaspoon savory
salt, pepper
2 eggs
2 lemons

Trim broad beans and cut in 2 or 3 pieces. Heat olive oil in a pot and sauté broad beans, fennel and garlic leaves for 5-10 minutes. Add savory, salt, pepper and water to cover them.
Cook until broad beans are soft. Turn off heat and prepare the egg-lemon sauce: Beat egg whites and continue with yolks, lemon juice and a little broth from the saucepan so that the temperature is balanced. Remove the pan from the heat and stir egg-lemon sauce into it.

Potatoes "savore" with rosemary

1 kilo potatoes
salt, 1 tbsp fresh rosemary
3-4 tbsp vinegar
olive oil for frying

Peel, rinse and cut potatoes into round slices, 2 cm thick. Dry them, sprinkle with salt and fry in olive oil until golden brown on both sides. When you have finished with the potatoes, turn off heat, pour vinegar carefully into the pan, add rosemary and pour the sauce over the potatoes. They are delicious either hot or cold.

Potatoes "betounges" with oregano

1 kilo small fresh potatoes
salt, 1 teaspoon oregano
½ cup olive oil

Wash potatoes and, without peeling them, boil in water for 10 minutes.

Peel them, sprinkle with salt and oregano and sauté in large, shallow pan until golden brown.

Stewed potatoes with herbs

1 kilo potatoes
½ cup olive oil
2 coarsely chopped onions
1 leek cut into rounds
2 finely chopped garlic cloves
½ kilo finely chopped tomatoes
1 sprig of thyme
2 bay leaves
2 sprigs of parsley
1 tbsp oregano
1 teaspoon grated orange rind
salt, pepper

Peel potatoes and cut in cubes.
Heat olive oil in a saucepan and sauté onion, leek, garlic, potatoes, thyme, bay leaves, parsley, orange rind and oregano. Stir carefully 2-3 times, pour in tomato, salt, pepper and water to cover everything and simmer until the sauce thickens.
Serve potatoes sprinkled with finely chopped parsley.

Courgette balls

1 kilo courgettes
2 eggs
1 small leek or fresh garlic, finely chopped
2 spring onions, finely chopped
1 cup finely chopped herbs
(dill, parsley, fennel, spearmint)
½ cup grated cheese or feta cheese
(optional)
   1 cup ground toasted bread or flour
   salt, pepper
   1 cup olive oil for frying

Right: Potatoes "betounges" with oregano.

Fried pumpkin pie

Grate courgettes, sprinkle with salt and place in a strainer to drain well. Combine with the rest of the ingredients.

Heat olive oil in a frying pan. Take spoonfuls from the mixture and pour in the hot oil. Fry until brown on both sides. (If the first spoonful of mixture spreads, add extra flour). Place the balls on kitchen roll to drain and serve.

Pumpkin balls

As above.

Substitute courgettes with pumpkin, which you first cut in cubes, boil in a little water for 10 minutes and strain well. It is also necessary to add 1 teaspoon cumin.

Left: Courgette balls

Fried pumpkin pie

2 cups pumpkin, grated and drained
1 grated onion
2 tbsp finely chopped parsley
2 tbsp finely chopped spearmint
1 egg
salt, pepper
4-5 tbsp ground toasted bread
4 tbsp olive oil

Grate pumpkin, season with salt and squeeze to remove excess liquid. Add onion, parsley, spearmint, beaten egg, pepper and toasted bread to thicken the mixture.

Heat olive oil in a pan and spread the pumpkin mixture.

When it has almost been cooked on one side, turn the pie over to be cooked on the other side.

♦ *Add a little grated cheese, if desired.*

Boiled mallows

1 kilo tender mallow shoots
½ cup olive oil
1 finely chopped onion
  2-3 mashed cloves of garlic
  salt, lemon juice

Trim mallows and keep only the tender tops. Wash them, put in boiling salted water and cook until soft. Strain and serve with the garlic, olive oil and lemon juice.

♦ *If desired, add 2 potatoes cut in slices.*

Vegetables on the grill with herbs

2 tomatoes
2 eggplants
2 green peppers
3-4 asparagus
1 onion
1 cup mushrooms
3 large courgettes
½ cup olive oil
1 cup finely chopped herbs (parsley, spearmint, oregano, basil)
salt, pepper

Wash vegetables and cut into medium round slices, except for the asparagus from which you remove only the fibrous part. In a bowl whisk olive oil with herbs and add vegetables. Leave them for 2 hours to marinate, turning on all sides from time to time to fully absorb the flavours. Take them out of the marinade, season with salt and cook on the grill brushing frequently with the marinade. Serve on a platter with herb leaves and freshly ground pepper.

♦ *You can accompany the vegetables with an aromatic yoghurt dip or sprinkle with grated cheese.*

Sofegada (mixed vegetables) in the oven

1 eggplant
2 courgettes
2 green peppers
3-4 small potatoes
1-2 finely chopped onions
2-3 finely chopped cloves of garlic
1 cup olive oil
½ kilo finely chopped tomatoes
2 bay leaves
2 tbsp finely chopped spearmint
2 tbsp finely chopped parsley
1 tbsp oregano, savory or thyme
salt, pepper

Clean and wash vegetables and cut into pieces. Place all ingredients in a baking dish, cover and cook in the oven for one hour. Uncover the dish and cook for another 20 minutes. *(Alternatively, you can first fry the vegetables slightly, then put in the baking dish, cover with sauce made with the tomatoes, the onion, the garlic and the herbs and cook in the oven for about half an hour.)*

Pie with flowered onion shoots

A specialty of the Greek emigrants from Asia Minor.

1 kilo flowered onion shoots
½ cup olive oil
5-6 eggs
For the batter:
½ kilo flour
2 cups water
½ cup olive oil
salt, pepper

Wash onion shoots, finely chop them, season with salt and squeeze to remove excess water. Add pepper, olive oil and beaten eggs and mix well.

Make a thick batter with the above ingredients and pour half of it in an oiled baking pan.

Spread the filling over the batter and cover with the remaining batter. Drizzle with a little olive oil and cook in the oven until the pie is golden brown.

ᝥ Oregano balls

½ kilo potatoes
1 egg
2-3 finely chopped spring onions
½ finely chopped fresh oregano
(dried oregano can be used as well)
½ cup ground toasted bread
salt, pepper
flour and olive oil for frying

Boil potatoes in water, peel and mash them. Mix with the onions, the beaten egg, salt, pepper and oregano. Place the mixture in the refrigerator for a while. Shape the balls, dredge in flour and fry in olive oil until brown on all sides. Place on absorbing paper to drain them.

♦ *(Instead of oregano, you can use other herbs, too, such as dill, fennel or parsley. You can also add grated cheese).*

ᝥ Mushroom pie with herbs

3-4 tbsp olive oil
1 finely chopped onion
½ kilo mushrooms
1 cup grated cheese
3 eggs
1 cup all-fat milk
2 tbsp herbs (spearmint, oregano, sage or parsley)
salt, pepper

Heat olive oil in a pan and sauté onion and mushroom for 10 minutes.

Add eggs and empty the mixture in an oiled baking pan. Beat eggs with the milk, herbs, salt and pepper and pour over the mushrooms. Bake in moderate heat until golden brown, 30-40 minutes.

♦ **Variation**: Add ½ cup calendula petals or saffron. Keep a few petals to decorate the pie.

ᝥ Baked mushrooms with herbs

½ kilo mushrooms
3-4 tbsp olive oil
½ cup white wine
4 tbsp finely chopped basil
2 tbsp thyme
salt, pepper

Rinse well and dry mushrooms. Place in a baking pan, pour the oil and wine over them, season with salt, pepper and the herbs and cook in the oven for 40-50 minutes.

♦ *If desired, add slices of potatoes or sprinkle with cheese.*

Oregano balls

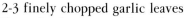

ᦸ Potato purée with chives and marjoram

1 kilo potatoes, boiled and peeled
3-4 tbsp olive oil
1 cup crumbled feta cheese
½ cup finely chopped chives
1 teaspoon marjoram
freshly ground pepper

Place all ingredients in the food processor and mix until mushy. Transfer into an oven-proof dish and cook in the oven for about half an hour.

♦ *You can leave feta cheese out and add 1 tbsp lemon juice.*

ᦸ Broccoli purée with basil

2 cups boiled broccoli
2 tbsp olive oil
2 garlic cloves
3 tbsp basil
2 tbsp lemon juice
3-4 tbsp grated cheese
3-4 tbsp chopped almonds
or walnuts
salt, pepper

For the preparation proceed as above.

ᦸ Sorrel pancakes

1 kilo chopped sorrel
3-4 finely chopped spring onions
2-3 finely chopped garlic leaves
½ cup finely chopped fennel
½ cup finely chopped cilantro or parsley
½ cup finely chopped spearmint
salt, pepper
1 cup olive oil for frying

Add salt and the juice of 2 bitter oranges to the herbs and rub them with your fingers to yield their juices. Add pepper and flour to make a thick batter.

Heat olive oil in a pan and add spoonfuls from the batter, one at a time. When the pancakes are brown on one side, turn them to cook on the other side.

ᦸ Fennel pancakes

1 cup finely chopped fennel
1 finely chopped spring onions
salt, pepper
1 cup water
1 cup flour
1 cup olive oil for frying

Make a batter with the water and the flour and combine with fennel, onion, salt and pepper.

Heat olive oil in a pan, take spoonfuls of batter and drop into the oil.

Cook pancakes until brown on both sides and place on absorbing paper before serving them.

Sorrel pancakes

⤳ Oregano pancakes

As above. Substitute fennel with half cup fresh oregano. If it is not available, use one tbsp dried oregano.

⤳ Pancakes with sun-dried tomatoes and fennel

1 cup sun-dried tomatoes
1 cup flour
2 tbsp finely chopped parsley
1 grated onion
2 tbsp finely chopped fennel
pepper
olive oil for frying

Soak dried tomatoes in water for a while to dissolve their salt and drain. Make a batter with the flour and one cup water and combine with parsley, onion, fennel and a little pepper.

Heat olive oil in a pan, dip sun-dried tomatoes, one at a time, in the batter and drop in the oil. Cook until brown on both sides and place on absorbing paper before serving.

Fennel pancakes

⤳ Omelet with vegetables and herbs

4 tbsp olive oil
1 finely chopped fresh onion
4 eggs
1 finely chopped tomato
1 finely chopped green pepper
1 cup chopped fresh herbs (chives, -blossoms as well-, chervil, tarragon, parsley, dill, oregano, basil)
If you do not have fresh herbs, you can substitute with half the amount of the dried herb.
1 tbsp chopped walnuts (optional)
salt, pepper

Heat olive oil in a skillet and sauté the onion and green pepper until soft. Beat the eggs in a bowl and add the herbs, walnuts, salt and

Oregano pancakes

pepper to taste. Pour the egg mixture in the skillet and allow the omelet to cook for a while. When one side is almost cooked through, turn it over and allow to be cooked on the other side. Serve immediately, sprinkled with chopped herbs.

Omelet with broccoli and spearmint

⤳ Poppy omelet

½ kilo tender shoots and leaves of poppy
2 finely chopped spring onions
2 tbsp finely chopped dill
2 tbsp finely chopped parsley
5-6 tbsp olive oil
4-5 eggs
salt, pepper

Blanch poppies in boiling water for 5-6 minutes and strain. Heat olive oil in a pan and sauté poppies until juice is evaporated. Add onion, parsley, dill, salt and pepper. Beat eggs and pour over the greens. When omelet is almost cooked on the one side, turn it over to be cooked on the other side.

⤳ Omelet with broccoli and spearmint or basil

As above. Use broccoli instead of poppies and spearmint or basil instead of dill. You can also add oregano, either dried or fresh.
♦ **Variation:** *Put the mixture in an ovenproof dish and cook the omelet in the oven until golden brown, about 50 minutes.*

⤳ Omelet with mallows

As above. Only the tender shoots from mallows are used.

⤳ Omelet with mustard flowers

1 cup mustard flowers
3 tbsp olive oil
3-4 eggs
salt, pepper
3 tbsp grated cheese (optional)

Heat olive oil in a pan. Beat eggs, add salt, pepper, the flowers and the cheese and pour the mixture in the pan.
When the bottom side of the omelet is golden brown, turn it over to be cooked on the other side.

⤳ Omelet with dandelion flowers

As above.

Right:
Omelet with mustard flowers

Omelet with chamomile flowers

❧ Omelet with chamomile flowers

As above.

❧ Omelet with tassel hyacinth flowers

As above.

❧ Eggplants stuffed with rice and herbs

The traveller Edward Brown, who visited Greece in 1669, was impressed by the way eggplants were cooked in Thessaly. He had never seen eggplants in his life and wrote that they were stuffed with herbs and were delicious.

1 kilo eggplants
2 dried onions or 4 spring onions, finely chopped
2 finely chopped cloves of garlic
1 teaspoon marjoram

Omelet with tassel hyacinth flowers

Artichoke pie

1 teaspoon thyme
1 cup finely chopped herbs
(basil, parsley, spearmint, dill or fennel)
½ kilo grated tomatoes
½ cup olive oil
1 cup rice
salt, pepper

Hollow eggplants, season with salt, both internally and externally, and set aside.
Combine the ingredients for the stuffing. Rinse eggplants, drain and stuff them. Place in a baking pan, drizzle with a little olive oil and cook in the oven until soft.

✑ Tomatoes stuffed with rice and herbs

As above.

✑ Artichoke pie

10 finely chopped artichoke hearts
2-3 finely chopped spring onions
2 tbsp finely chopped parsley

2 tbsp finely chopped dill
4 tbsp olive oil
2 tbsp flour
1 cup milk
2 eggs
200 grams feta cheese
100 grams grated "kefalotyri" cheese
salt, pepper

Heat 2 tablespoons olive oil in a pan and sauté onions, artichokes, parsley and dill for 3-4 minutes. Add 1 cup of water, salt and pepper and cook until water is evaporated.
Prepare the cream: Heat remaining olive oil in a saucepan, add flour, stir a couple of times and then pour in hot milk, little by little, stirring constantly until the mixture thickens. Turn off the heat and stir in beaten eggs, cheese, a little salt and pepper. Transfer to a baking pan and bake in moderate heat until golden brown.
◆ *If desired, spread a sheet of phyllo dough on the bottom of the baking pan.*

⌇ Byzantine "aghiozoumi"

4 tbsp olive oil
1 grated onion
2 tbsp vinegar
salt, 1 teaspoon savory
2 slices stale bread (preferably toasted)

Whisk olive oil and vinegar.
   Place bread on a platter, drizzle with olive oil and vinegar and season with salt and savory.

⌇ "Riganatha"

"Riganatha" of the Ionian islands is very much like the Byzantine "aghiozoumi". The kind of vinegar used is "triantaphyloxitho" (vinegar scented with rose petals) and the herb is of course oregano, as the name itself indicates.
◆**Variation:** *Rub a mixture of herbs over the slices of bread, such as parsley, basil, marjoram, savory or thyme.*

⌇ Zahtar

Zahtar, the well known mixture of the Middle East, is similar to "aghiozoumi" and "riganatha":
Use slices of bread or thin bread pies, drizzle with olive oil and toast on the grill for 5 minutes. Season with mashed garlic, thyme, sesame seeds and salt.

⌇ Slices of bread with tomato and basil

As above. Add grated tomato and basil.

◆ *Apart from basil, you can also use parsley, fennel, chervil, marjoram, oregano, rosemary or grated lemon zest.*

⌇ Slices of bread with herbs and cheese

½ kilo of bread cut into 8 slices
4 tbsp olive oil
2 tbsp finely chopped parsley
1 tbsp oregano
1 cup grated cheese

Toast bread slices on the grill for 5 minutes. Sprinkle with olive oil, parsley, oregano and cheese. Cook again until the cheese melts.

⌇ Crutons with herbs for soups or salads

250 grams cut into cubes
3 tbsp olive oil
1 mashed clove of garlic
3 tbsp finely chopped herbs
(oregano, thyme, marjoram, basil, parsley)
salt

Heat olive oil in a pan with garlic and herbs for 1-2 minutes. Add bread and a little salt and brown lightly on all sides.

These croutons are ideal in soups or in salads.

PULSES

✎ Split pea purée with herbs

½ kilo split peas
½ cup olive oil
1 finely chopped onion
1 carrot cut into dice
2 leeks cut into rounds
½ cup finely chopped parsley
½ cup finely chopped chervil
or Venus' combs
1 cup coarsely chopped sorrel
salt, pepper

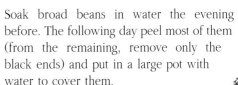

Soak split peas in water the evening before. The following day heat olive oil in a pot and sauté onion, leeks and carrot for 5 minutes. Add drained split peas, parsley, sorrel, chervil and 1 liter water and simmer for about one hour without covering the pot and stirring frequently so that the food doesn't stick to the bottom of the pot and becomes mushy.
Serve garnished with herb leaves.

✎ Dried broad bean purée with herbs

½ kilo dried broad beans
2 tbsp finely chopped parsley
5-6 mashed cloves of garlic
1 tbsp marjoram
1 tbsp finely chopped spearmint
salt, olive oil

Soak broad beans in water the evening before. The following day peel most of them (from the remaining, remove only the black ends) and put in a large pot with water to cover them.
Boil until cooked and the water has evaporated. Towards the end stir constantly so that they don't stick to the bottom of the pot and become mushy. Serve with olive oil and the herbs.

✎ Lentil soup with herbs

½ kilo lentils
½ cup olive oil
1 onion, finely chopped
3 finely chopped cloves of garlic
½ kilo finely chopped tomatoes
2 carrots, diced
3 tbsp finely chopped celery
2 bay leaves
1 tbsp thyme
1 tbsp savory
3 tbsp vinegar
salt, pepper

Boil lentils in a large pot with plenty of water for 10-15 minutes and transfer to a colander. Heat the olive oil in the same pot and sauté onion, garlic, carrot and celery for 5 minutes.
Add bay leaves, thyme, savory, tomatoes, lentils, salt, pepper and 3-4 cups water. Boil

until lentils are cooked, about half an hour. Stir in vinegar 5 minutes before the food is ready.

✎ Lentil soup with orange peel

As above. In this variation flavour is enriched with the peel of 1 orange.
You can omit salt and add 2 salted anchovies shortly before lentils are cooked.

½ cup finely chopped parsley
½ cup finely chopped celery
½ cup finely chopped fennel
1 teaspoon oregano
½ kilo grated tomatoes
salt, pepper

Soak lima beans in water the evening before. The following day boil them in plenty of water until soft and strain. Heat olive oil in a saucepan and sauté vegetables and herbs for 5 minutes. Add tomatoes and cook for 10 more minutes. Put beans and greens in a pan, season with salt and pepper, add a little water and cook in the oven for another half hour.

✎ Dried bean purée

½ kilo dried beans
½ cup olive oil
the juice of 1 lemon
3 tbsp finely chopped dill
3 tbsp finely chopped parsley
1 finely chopped spring onion
salt, pepper or ½ hot pepper

✎ Large lima beans with vegetables and herbs

½ kilo lima beans
½ cup olive oil
1 leek cut into rounds
1 finely chopped onion
½ kilo coarsely chopped spinach
½ kilo coarsely chopped white beet leaves

Boil dried beans in plenty of water until soft. Mash them in the food processor together with the hot pepper and combine with the rest of the ingredients. Add a little juice from the pot to make a smooth purée. Garnish with sage leaves.

♦ *You can also add savory, basil, oregano or marjoram.*

Right:
Lentil soup with herbs

SNAILS

☙ Snails with Venus' combs and fennel

½ kilo snails
½ cup olive oil
1 kilo potatoes cut in quarters
1 finely chopped onion
2 cups finely chopped Venus' combs
2 cups finely chopped fennel
the juice of 1 lemon
salt, pepper

Put snails in a pot, cover with water and bring to the boil. Clean and rinse them well. Heat olive oil in a pan and brown onion for 5 minutes. Add snails, Venus' combs, fennel and potatoes and stir a couple of times. Pour in 2-3 cups water and cook until most water has evaporated. Add lemon juice 5 minutes before turning off the heat.

☙ Snails with wild artichokes, fennel and fresh almonds

1 kilo wild artichoke leaves or hearts
½ cup olive oil
1 cup finely chopped dill or fennel
½ cup finely chopped garlic or spring onion leaves or chives
½ kilo snails
½ kilo fresh almonds
salt, pepper
juice of 1 lemon

Put snails in a pot, cover with water and bring to the boil. Clean and rinse them well. Clean artichokes (remove the thorns) and rinse them well. Boil them in ample water for 10 minutes and then strain. Heat olive oil in a pot and sauté

garlic or onion and fennel for 5 minutes. Add snails, artichokes, almonds, salt and 1-2 cups water and cook for half an hour.
Finally add lemon juice and pepper and turn off the heat.

☙ Snails with Spanish oyster plants

As above. Leave out the almonds and add 2-3 medium potatoes cut in quarters.

☙ Snails with herbs in tomato sauce

1 kilo snails
½ cup olive oil
1 kilo potatoes cut in quarters
2 coarsely chopped onions
2-3 cloves of garlic, finely chopped
½ kilo finely chopped tomatoes
a bunch of herbs (marjoram, thyme, mint, bay leaves, parsley)
salt, pepper

Put snails in a pot, cover with water and bring to the boil.
Clean and rinse them well.
Heat olive oil in a pan and sauté onion for 5 minutes. Add snails, garlic and potatoes and sauté 5 more minutes.
Pour in tomato, 2-3 cups of hot water, add the bunch of herbs, salt and pepper and simmer until the sauce thickens.

☙ Snails with black bryony or asparagus

1 kilo snails
1 kilo black bryony or asparagus

Snails with wild artichokes, fennel and fresh almonds

½ cup olive oil
1 finely chopped onion
1 cup finely chopped fennel
½ cup wine
½ kilo grated tomatoes
salt, pepper

Trim asparagus or black bryony, remove the tough parts and blanch them in boiling water for 5 minutes. Then strain.

Prepare snails: Put them in a pot, cover with water and bring to the boil. Clean and rinse them well.

Heat olive oil in a saucepan and sauté onion, snails and fennel for 10 minutes. Pour in wine and tomato and cook for another 10 minutes.

Add black bryony or asparagus, salt, pepper and 1 cup water. Simmer until the sauce thickens, about 20 minutes.

Snails with black bryony and fennel.

FISH - SEA FOOD

☞ Corsican bouillabaisse

2-3 kilos fish
(marine eel, red mullet, pike etc.)
2-3 potatoes in wedges
For the broth:
the heads and tails of the fish
1 onion cut into rounds
1 leek cut into rounds
4 finely chopped cloves of garlic
5-6 tbsp olive oil
2 tomatoes cut in quarters
1 bunch of herbs (parsley,
bay leaves, thyme, savory)
the peel of 1 orange
2 hot peppers
2 liters water
salt, pepper
the juice of 1 lemon
5-6 saffron stamens (optional)

Clean, gut and rinse
fish well.
Cut off heads and tails and put aside for the broth.

◆ **Prepare the broth:** Put water in a large
pot and bring to the boil. Add onion, leek,
garlic, tomatoes, olive oil, herbs, orange
peel, hot peppers and the heads and tails of
the fish. Boil over high heat for 15-20 minutes. Pass the broth through a sieve and put
it back into the pot.
Bring to the boil again, add potatoes, saffron
and fish and boil for another 20 minutes.
Finally pour in lemon juice and turn off the
heat.

☞ Fish with fennel
and saffron in tomato sauce

1 kilo fish (mullet, parrot fish,
red mullet or large fish in slices)

For the marinade:
½ cup white wine
½ teaspoon saffron
1 tbsp ground fennel seeds
the juice of 1 lemon
salt, pepper

For the sauce:
4 tbsp olive oil
1 finely chopped onion
½ cup finely chopped fennel
1 finely chopped garlic clove
½ kilo tomatoes
1 teaspoon oregano or thyme
1 bay leaf, salt, pepper

The evening before place fish in a
large bowl and cover with the
marinade. The following day heat
olive oil in a pan and sauté onion
and fennel for 5 minutes.
Add garlic, the marinade, the
herbs, salt and pepper and cook
for another 10 minutes.

Place fish over the herbs, cover with the tomato and simmer for 15-20 more minutes, shaking the pot from time to time.

◆ **Variation:** Stuff fish with finely chopped fennel, season with salt, pepper and thyme, drizzle with olive oil and lemon juice and cook in the oven for about 50 minutes.

☞ Baked fish with rosemary

1 kilo fish (mackerel, horse-mackerel, pike, mullet, etc.)
1 finely chopped onion
4-5 tbsp olive oil
1 finely chopped clove of garlic
½ kilo finely chopped tomatoes
2 tbsp vinegar
2 tbsp rosemary
salt, pepper

Brown onion in the oil, add garlic, tomatoes, vinegar and rosemary and cook for 10 minutes.
Place fish in an oiled baking pan, cover with the sauce and cook in the oven for about 50 minutes.

☞ Fish in the oven with thyme

1 kilo fish (sole, pike, red snapper etc.)
grated zest and juice of 1 lemon
1 tbsp thyme
6 tbsp olive oil
salt, pepper

Clean and gut fish and sprinkle with salt, pepper, lemon zest, thyme and 3 tbsp olive oil, both inside and outside.
Place on oiled baking pan, drizzle with remaining olive oil and lemon juice and bake at moderate heat.

ᴥ Fish on the grill with herbs

Prepare the fish as above. Place on grill and cook for about 20 minutes turning it once when it is done on one side. You can serve the fish on a platter, on thyme sprigs and accompany with a herb dressing (made with olive oil, lemon juice, thyme, finely chopped lemon balm or basil and a little salt).

ᴥ Fish in the oven on lemon or myrtle leaves

The fish is prepared as above. Place the fish in the baking pan over a layer of lemon or myrtle leaves. Serve with 2-3 lemon blossoms.

ᴥ Sardines with green peppers and sage

1 kilo sardines
2-3 green peppers cut into rounds
5-6 sage leaves

3-4 tbsp olive oil
salt, pepper

Clean and gut sardines and place in baking pan over the peppers. Season with salt, pepper and sage, drizzle with olive oil and cook in the oven for 50-60 minutes.

ᴥ Fish balls with parsley and dill

½ kilo fresh fish or salted cod
1 grated dried onion
1 finely chopped spring onion
2 tbsp finely chopped parsley
2 tbsp finely chopped dill
3 tbsp olive oil
1 cup flour
1 cup milk
2 eggs
salt, pepper
olive oil for frying

Fillet fish and cut into small pieces. (If you use salted cod, put it first in water for 12-15 hours to dissolve the salt changing the water 4-5 times).
Heat olive oil in a pan and sauté onions for 3-4 minutes.
Add flour, stir a couple of times and then pour in hot milk, stirring constantly. Add fish, salt and pepper and cook for 10 more minutes. Turn off the heat, stir in the eggs and the parsley and let the mixture cool down. Shape the fish balls, dredge in flour and fry in olive oil until golden brown on all sides.

♦ *You can also take spoonfuls of the mixture and drop them in the oil to be fried. Drain on absorbing paper before serving.*

Right: Fish in the oven on lemon or myrtle leaves

✎ Tuna fish
on the grill with lavender

1 kilo tuna fish cut into slices
½ cup lavender blossoms
½ cup fennel
3-4 tbsp olive oil
salt, pepper

Prepare the marinade with the above ingredients and marinade the fish for one hour. Cook on the grill for a few minutes on each side.

✎ Salmon with dill

1 kilo salmon in slices
3 tbsp olive oil
½ cup white wine
salt, pepper
½ cup dill

Prepare marinade with wine, salt, pepper and dill and marinate salmon for one hour. Take salmon out of the marinade and place in oiled baking tin. Cook in moderate oven for about half an hour.

✎ Fish wrapped in vine leaves

The custom to cook fish or seafood wrapped in vine leaves was known from antiquity. Antiphanes (2nd c. B.C.) mentions tuna fish wrapped in beet leaves, Kleostratus (4th c. B.C.) refers to fish with oregano wrapped in fig leaves and cooked in the ashes and the poet Ananius (6th c. B.C.) praises shrimps wrapped in fig leaves.

1 kilo fish (anchovies, sardines, red mullet, tuna fish or filleted large fish)
as many vine leaves as the fish
1 tbsp fresh oregano or thyme
2 tbsp finely chopped parsley
2 tbsp finely chopped dill
salt, pepper
2 lemons, 3 tbsp olive oil

Clean and gut fish. Put in a bowl, drizzle with olive oil, lemon juice, herbs, salt and pepper and leave in the refrigerator for 3-4 hours.
Blanch vine leaves in boiling water for 2-3 minutes and wrap fish in them. Place fish wrapped in vine leaves on oiled baking tin, drizzle with the marinade and cook in the oven for about half an hour.

✎ Sun-dried fish
with dittany

The most suitable fish for this preparation is mackerel or minnow.
1 kilo fish
salt, pepper
1-2 tbsp dittany leaves
3 tbsp olive oil

Clean and gut fish and remove the central bone. Rub with salt and a little olive oil, stuff with a little dittany and hang in the sun to dry. Cook on charcoals for 2-3 minutes on each side. Drizzle with lemon juice and serve.

✎ Squid stuffed with spinach

1 kilo squid
For the stuffing: 250 grams spinach
5 tbsp olive oil
1 dried onion or 4 spring onions, finely chopped
½ cup finely chopped herbs
(parsley, basil, spearmint)
½ cup rice
salt, pepper

and cook for 5-10 minutes.

Pour the sauce over the squid and bake in moderate heat for about three quarters of an hour.

Salted cod with fresh oregano

For the tomato sauce: 2 tbsp olive oil
1 finely chopped onion
2 finely chopped garlic cloves
2 grated tomatoes
½ cup white wine
1 tbsp finely chopped parsley

Prepare squid: remove intestines, eyes and the jelly bone. Rinse well and cut off the tentacles.

Clean, rinse and chop spinach. Heat olive oil in a pan and sauté onion and tentacles for 10-15 minutes. Add spinach and herbs and sauté for another 10 minutes.

Turn off heat and stir in rice, salt and pepper. Stuff the squid, taking care not to overfill them, and place in baking tin.

Prepare the sauce: Heat olive oil and sauté onion and garlic. Add remaining ingredients

☜ Salted cod with fresh oregano

1 kilo salted cod
1 kilo greens suitable for stew (Venus' combs, spinach, fennel, wild leeks etc.)
1,5 cup fresh oregano
1 dried onion or 2-3 spring onions, finely chopped
1 tbsp tomato paste dissolved in 1 cup water
1 potato cut in wedges
little salt, pepper

The day before cut cod into portions and soak in water to dissolve its salt. Change the water 4-5 times. The following day rinse and chop greens, blanch in boiling water for 5 minutes and strain. Blanch oregano for 2 minutes and strain, too.

Heat olive oil in a saucepan and sauté greens for 10 minutes.

Add tomato paste, potato, cod, oregano, pepper and water to cover the food. Cook until the sauce thickens, about half an hour, without stirring the food, only shaking the pan form time to time.

If it is necessary, season with a little salt.

◆ *This dish has a unique taste and flavour owing to the fresh oregano.*

Stewed octopus
with oregano and fennel

1 kilo octopus
½ cup olive oil
2 finely chopped onions
½ cup finely chopped fennel
2-3 bay leaves
1 kilo potatoes
1 tbsp tomato paste dissolved in 1 cup water or ½ kilo grated tomatoes
salt, pepper
1 tbsp oregano

Wash octopus, cut in pieces and put in a casserole.
Cook until its liquid has evaporated and then pour in olive oil. As soon as it is hot, add onion, fennel, potatoes, tomato paste, bay leaves, a little salt (the octopus itself doesn't need any salt), pepper, oregano and 2-3 cups water. Simmer until the sauce thickens and the food is cooked.

Squid with herbs
in tomato sauce

As above. Leave potatoes out and accompany with simple rice pilaf. You can enrich the flavour of the dish with the peel of one orange.

Mussels
with lemon balm

1 kilo mussels
3 tbsp olive oil
3 tbsp lemon balm

Cockles with savory

1 finely chopped onion
2 finely chopped garlic cloves
½ cup white wine
salt, pepper

Heat olive oil in a pan and sauté lemon balm for 2 minutes to release its aroma.
Add onion and garlic and sauté for another 2 minutes. Pour in wine, 1 cup hot water and, after 3-4 minutes, the mussels.
Cook for another 5-6 minutes and discard the mussels which have not opened. Add salt and pepper and turn off heat.

Cockles with savory

As above.
Use savory instead of lemon balm.

MEAT

❧ "Mageiritsa" with spearmint

    liver from a lamb or kid
    mall intestines (optional)
    olive oil
5-6 fresh onions, finely chopped
1 tbsp fresh oregano leaves
½ cup finely chopped parsley
1,5 cup finely chopped fresh
spearmint
1 tbsp tomato paste
salt, pepper

Wash and chop liver and intestines.
Heat olive oil in a pot and sauté onions and
innards until all liquid has evaporated.
Add oregano, parsley, spearmint and tomato
diluted in 1 cup water and cook for another
15-20 minutes.
♦ *You can add egg-lemon sauce.*

❧ Rooster cooked with cheese and herbs

1 rooster
    6 tbsp olive oil
    2 coarsely chopped onions
    1 finely chopped clove of garlic
    1 finely chopped tomato and 1 tbsp
    tomato paste diluted in 1 cup water
    1 bunch of herbs
    (bay leaves, parsley, thyme,
    oregano)
2-3 potatoes (optional)
½ kilo gruyere cheese
salt, pepper

Wash rooster and cut into portions.
Heat olive oil in a pan and sauté rooster on
all sides.
Add onions and brown lightly. Pour in fresh
tomato and tomato paste, garlic, herbs, salt,

pepper and 2 cups water and cook for 1 hour shaking the pan from time to time.
Add the cheese cut into cubes and turn off the heat.

~ Chicken or turkey stuffed with fruit

1 big chicken
salt, pepper
2 tbsp olive oil
1 onion cut into rounds
2 finely chopped cloves
of garlic
1 cup chopped prunes
1 cup chopped apples
1 cup chopped dried apricots
½ cup raisins
1 teaspoon cinnamon powder
1 teaspoon grated orange zest
1 tbsp sugar
½ cup orange juice

Wash chicken and season with salt.
Heat olive oil in a skillet and sauté onion and garlic for 2 minutes. Add fruits, salt, pepper, orange zest, cinnamon and 2-3 tbsp water and stir. Stuff chicken, close with toothpicks and place in a baking pan. Pour orange juice over it and bake in moderate heat for 2-3

hours, brushing the chicken occasionally with the juice from the pan. Serve with rice pilaf.

♦ *In the same way you can cook turkey stuffed with fruit.*

~ Guinea hen or chicken with figs and thyme

1 guinea-hen or chicken
cut into portions
½ kilo figs
1 teaspoon dried thyme
or 1 tbsp fresh thyme
2 finely chopped onions
2 finely chopped garlic cloves
½ cup white wine
5 tbsp olive oil
salt, pepper

Wash guinea hen or chicken and sauté in olive oil until brown on all sides. Add onion and sauté for 5 more minutes.
Pour in wine, figs, 1-2 cups hot water, season with salt and pepper and simmer until the meat is soft and the sauce is thick.
Flavour with thyme shortly before turning off the heat.

Chicken with saffron or calendula petals

2 boneless chicken breasts
cut into small pieces
4 tbsp olive oil
1 onion, finely chopped
½ kilo finely chopped tomatoes
5-6 saffron stamens
or ½ cup calendula petals
1 tbsp sugar
2 cups rice
salt, pepper

In a large skillet heat olive oil and brown chicken on all sides for 10 minutes. Remove the chicken and add the rice and onion to the skillet. Cook stirring constantly for 5 minutes and then pour in 2-3 cups water, tomato, saffron stamens or calendula petals, salt and pepper. When it gets back to the boil, return the chicken to the skillet and simmer until tender, for about 15-20 more minutes.

◆ **Variation**: Add ½ cup chopped almonds and ½ cup raisins.

Chicken with yoghurt and saffron

1 medium chicken cut into portions
½ cup olive oil
2 finely chopped garlic cloves
1 tbsp ground coriander seeds
1 cup yoghurt
the juice of 1 lemon
1 teaspoon grated orange or lemon rind
½ grated hot pepper
1 teaspoon grated ginger
½ teaspoon saffron stamens
salt, pepper

Wash chicken and place in a large bowl mixed with yoghurt and the rest of the ingredients. Let it stand in the refrigerator for one night.

Chicken with saffron

Turkey fillets stuffed with Venus' combs

The following day transfer the chicken mixture into a baking pan, cover with aluminum foil and bake initially at a high heat for half an hour and then at medium heat for another hour and a half.

◆ **Variation**: The chicken with its marinade can be cooked in the casserole as well.

☙ Chicken or turkey fillets with Venus' combs

4 chicken or turkey fillets
4 spring onions, finely chopped
4 tbsp olive oil
2 mashed garlic cloves
1 cup finely chopped Venus' comb and ivory-fruited hartwort
½ cup white wine
salt, pepper

Season fillets with salt and pepper. Mix remaining ingredients and

share the mixture on the fillets. Wrap the mixture in the fillets, close with toothpicks and sauté the rolls in olive oil until brown on all sides. Pour in wine, transfer to a baking pan and bake at moderate heat until soft.

☙ Turkey stuffed with herbs

1 medium turkey
½ cup olive oil
2 finely chopped onions
zest and juice of 1 lemon and 1 orange
½ cup white wine
1 tbsp thyme
1 tbsp marjoram
2 tbsp finely chopped parsley
1 teaspoon sage leaves
salt, pepper
1 cup rice

Using a mortar and pestle mush all herbs and spices together.

Add the wine, lemon juice and orange juice and combine well.

Wash turkey and brush with half the herb and spice mixture.

Heat olive oil in a skillet and sauté onion until translucent. Add the remaining herb and spice mixture and 3 cups water. When it comes to the boil, stir in rice and cook for 5-6 minutes. Turn off heat, let the rice absorb all the water and stuff the turkey with this mixture.

Place turkey in a baking pan, cover with aluminum foil and roast at low to medium heat for 3-4 hours, brushing it frequently with its juices. Towards the end, remove the foil so that the turkey turns golden brown.

Duck with orange juice

1 duck
5-6 tbsp olive oil
2 cups orange juice
the juice of 2 lemons
3-4 tbsp brandy
1 cinnamon stick
the peel of 1 orange
and 1 lemon
1 teaspoon sage leaves
1 teaspoon fennel seeds
salt, pepper

Wash duck and cut into portions. Heat olive oil in a skillet and sauté duck for 5 minutes. Pour in brandy, orange and lemon juice. Season with salt, pepper, cinnamon, lemon and orange peel, sage and fennel seeds and simmer until the meat is tender and the sauce is thick.

Rabbit in wine with peppers and basil

1 rabbit
½ kilo peppers cut into strips
½ cup olive oil

3 finely chopped tomatoes
2 finely chopped onions
2 finely chopped garlic cloves
1 cup white wine
1 teaspoon dried basil
or 1 tbsp fresh basil
salt, pepper

Rabbit with sage and grapes

Wash rabbit, cut into portions and season with salt and pepper.

Heat olive oil in a large skillet and brown rabbit on all sides.

Add onion and garlic, sauté for another 5 minutes and pour in wine. Cover the skillet, simmer for 15 minutes and then add tomatoes, basil, peppers, salt and pepper. Simmer until rabbit is soft.

⌒ Rabbit with sage and grapes

1 rabbit (partridges, quails or pigeons can also be used)
½ cup olive oil
1 finely chopped onion
1 cup white wine
2 sprigs of sage
the juice of ½ lemon
salt, pepper
½ cup grapes

Cut the rabbit into portions, wash and sauté in olive oil until brown on all sides. Add onion, brown it and pour in the wine. Add sage, salt and pepper, cover the pot and simmer until rabbit is soft.
Remove rabbit with a perforated spoon and pour lemon juice and grapes into the sauce. Simmer for 3-4 minutes and pour the sauce over the rabbit.

⌒ Rabbit with herbs in egg-lemon sauce

1 rabbit
1,5 cup white wine
1 bunch of herbs (savory, rosemary, oregano, thyme, bay leaves)
5-6 tbsp olive oil
1 finely chopped dried onion
2-3 spring onions, finely chopped
2 garlic cloves, finely chopped
1 cup finely chopped parsley
1 egg, 2 lemons

Prepare a marinade with the wine and the herbs. Cut rabbit into portions, wash it, season with salt and pepper and marinate for 3-4 hours.
Remove rabbit from the marinade and sauté in olive oil until brown on all sides. Add onion, garlic and, after 5 minutes, the parsley and water to cover the rabbit.
Cover the pot and simmer for 50 minutes, until rabbit is soft. Turn off heat and prepare the egg-lemon sauce: Beat egg white and

continue with yolks, lemon juice and a little broth from the saucepan so that the temperature is balanced. Remove the pan from the heat and stir egg-lemon sauce into it.

Lamb with asparagus in flour-lemon sauce or egg-lemon sauce

1 kilo meat
1 kilo asparagus (wild or cultivated)
1 cup Venus' combs or wild carrots, finely chopped
2 tbsp finely chopped dill
½ cup olive oil
2 spring onions, finely chopped
½ cup white wine
1 lemon
1 tbsp flour
salt, pepper
oregano or thyme

Wash meat and cut into chunks. Heat olive oil in a large skillet and brown onion for 2-3 minutes. Add meat and brown it on all sides. Pour in wine and 2 cups of water and cook until meat is soft, about 40 minutes.
Trim asparagus leaving only the tender part, wash them, drain and add to the meat. Season wih salt and pepper, pour in a little water, if needed, and cook for another 10 minutes. Dilute flour in a little broth from the skillet, add lemon and pour the mixture into the skillet. Shake the skillet and cook for 5 more minutes.

Page192: Rabbit with herbs in egg-lemon sauce.
Page 193: Meat with lemon, oregano and lemon balm

♦ *If you prefer egg-lemon sauce, use 1 egg instead of the flour and prepare the sauce as in the above recipe.*

Meat with sorrel in egg-lemon sauce

As above. Use sorrel instead of asparagus.

Meat with wild artichokes or Spanish oyster plants

As above. Use 1 kilo wild artichokes or Spanish oyster plants or both.

Meat with oregano and lemon balm

1,5 kilo meat (lamb, kid, chicken or rabbit)
3-4 tbsp olive oil
the juice of 2 lemons
3-4 fresh tops of lemon shoots or 2 tbsp lemon balm
1 tbsp oregano
salt, pepper

Wash meat, cut into chunks and season with salt and pepper.
Heat olive oil in a pan and brown meat on all sides. Add lemon juice, lemon balm and oregano, cover the pan and simmer until the meat is soft, adding a little water if needed.
♦ *You can add a few potatoes cut into quarters.*

Lamb with spinach and dried fruit

✎ Stuffed kid or lamb from the island of Karpathos

1 small kid or lamb
2 lemons
4-5 tbsp olive oil

For the filling:
½ cup olive oil
6-7 spring onions, finely chopped
the liver of the animal, finely chopped
½ cup finely chopped dill
½ kilo finely chopped tomatoes
2 cups rice
salt, pepper

Heat olive oil in a pot and sauté onions and liver for 5 minutes. Add dill and tomato and cook for another 5 minutes. Stir in rice, season with salt and pepper and turn off the heat.
Wash lamb or kid, season with salt and pepper both inside and outside and stuff with the mixture, to which you add 1 cup water.

Close with toothpicks, place in a large baking tin, brush with olive oil and lemon, cover with aluminum foil and bake at a high temperature at the beginning and then at medium heat for about 3 hours or more.
Uncover towards the end so that the meat turns brown.

✎ Lamb with spinach and dried fruit

1 kilo boneless lamb cut into cubes
6 tbsp olive oil
1 finely chopped onion
½ kilo spinach, chopped coarsely
1 leek cut into rounds
3 finely chopped spring onions
½ cup finely chopped dill
the juice of 2 lemons
salt, pepper
1 cup dried fruit
(prunes, apricots or plums)

Lamb in meat sauce

Heat half olive oil in a large skillet and sauté onion and meat until brown on all sides. Cover with water and cook for about one hour.

Heat remaining olive oil in another skillet and sauté leek and fresh onions for 3 minutes. Add spinach and sauté for another 10 minutes. Mix with the meat, season with salt, pepper and lemon juice and cook for another 10-15 minutes.

Add dill and fruit 5 minutes before turning off the heat. Serve with rice pilaf.

Lamb in the oven with thyme

1,5 kilo meat (lamb or kid)
cut into portions
3-4 tbsp olive oil
1 cup white wine
1 tbsp thyme
salt, pepper

Wash lamb and place in a large bowl with the wine and the thyme for one night.
The following day, season it with salt, pepper and olive oil, place in a baking pan and cook in the oven until meat is separated from the bone.

Lamb in mint sauce

1 kilo leg of lamb cut into portions
4 tbsp olive oil
2 crushed cloves of garlic
½ cup white wine
1 cup fresh mint leaves,
chopped coarsely
salt and pepper to taste
3 tbsp fresh mint leaves, chopped finely

Wash and dry lamb. Season with the garlic, salt and pepper.
Heat olive oil in a pan and sauté the lamb until browned on all sides.
Transfer to a baking pan and bake

until soft. Pour the wine into the pan where you sautéed the lamb and let it simmer for a few minutes.

Add 1 cup water and the coarsely chopped mint. Simmer for 10-15 minutes, then strain. Add the finely chopped mint to the sauce, pour it over the lamb and serve.

✑ Pork cooked in the oven with thyme and sage

1,5 kilo pork leg
4 tbsp olive oil
2 tbsp lemon juice
4 tbsp orange juice
1 cup white wine
2 sprigs of thyme
2 sprigs of marjoram
2 sprigs of sage
salt, pepper

Wash meat, incise and insert thyme, marjoram and sage leaves in the incisions. Season with salt and pepper and drizzle with olive oil, orange juice, lemon juice and wine. Let it stand in the marinade for 2-3 hours, turning it on all sides from to time to time to marinate well.

Transfer to a baking pan and bake at moderate heat until soft and browned.

✑ Meat with eggplants and herbs

1 kilo meat (lamb, pork or veal)
5 tbsp olive oil
2 finely chopped onions
½ kilo courgettes cut into rounds
½ kilo eggplants cut into cubes
1 teaspoon thyme
1 teaspoon savory
1 tbsp rosemary
2 tbsp finely chopped fresh dill
½ kilo finely chopped tomatoes
salt, pepper

Pork cooked in the oven with thyme and sage.

Goat with herbs in tomato sauce.

Wash meat and cut into cubes. Heat half olive oil in a skillet and brown meat on all sides. Cover with water and simmer for one hour.

Heat remaining olive oil in another skillet and sauté onions, courgettes and eggplants for a few minutes.

Add tomatoes and empty the content of this skillet over the meat. Season with the herbs, salt and pepper, stir carefully and cook for another 10-15 minutes.

∽ Goat with herbs in tomato sauce

1,5 kilo goat cut into small portions
1-2 finely chopped onions
2-3 finely chopped garlic cloves
5-6 tbsp olive oil
½ cup red wine
1 kilo finely chopped tomatoes
a bunch of herbs (thyme, bay leaves, rosemary, parsley)
salt, pepper

Heat olive oil in a pot and sauté goat, onions and garlic for a few minutes. Pour in wine, cover with water and cook for one hour. Add tomato, herbs, salt and pepper and simmer until goat is soft and the sauce is thick.

∽ Pork with thyme and vinegar

1 kilo boneless pork cut in dice
1 tbsp thyme
5-6 mashed garlic cloves
2 tbsp olive oil
1 cup vinegar
salt, pepper

Whisk vinegar with thyme, garlic, salt and pepper.

Put meat in the marinade and let it stand in the refrigerator for 2-3 days.

Transfer the meat with the marinade into a pot and simmer until liquid is evaporated. Then add olive oil and cook meat until soft and brown on all sides.

∽ Meat in the oven with lentisk seeds

1,5 kilo meat (pork or lamb), preferably from leg
1 kilo potatoes
2 tomatoes cut into slices
3 garlic cloves cut in slices
4-5 tbsp olive oil
1 tbsp lentisk seeds
salt, pepper

Wash meat, make incisions, insert garlic and lentisk seeds in the incisions and brush with olive oil, salt and pepper.

Peel the potatoes, cut them in slices, season with salt and pepper and arrange around the meat in the baking pan. Cover with tomato slices, add a little water and cook at moderate heat until soft and brown.

♦ **Variation**: Instead of tomato, you can use zest and juice of 1-2 lemons.

∽ Wild boar with chestnuts and herbs

1 kilo wild boar or pork cut in cubes
1,5 cup red wine
½ cup tsikoudia (alcoholic drink)
1 kilo chestnuts
2 fennel sprigs
5-6 tbsp olive oil
1 finely chopped onion
2 finely chopped garlic cloves
a bunch of herbs
(parsley, bay leaves, thyme, rosemary)
salt, pepper

Prepare the marinade with the onion, garlic,

herbs (bouquet garni), wine, tsikoudia and pepper. Put meat in the marinade and leave it there for 24 hours.

Incise chestnuts, boil in salted water with the fennel for 10 minutes and peel carefully to allow them to remain whole.

Take meat out of the marinade and sauté in a pot with olive oil until browned on all sides.

Pour in the marinade, salt and a little pepper and simmer for about 2 hours, adding a little hot water, if needed.

Finally add chestnuts and cook for another 15 minutes, without stirring, only shake the pot from time to time so that chestnuts are not crushed.

♦ *You can use pork instead of wild boar.*

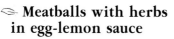

◁ Meatballs with herbs in egg-lemon sauce

½ kilo minced meat (from pork and lamb or veal)
1 dried onion or 3 fresh onions, finely chopped
1 egg
1 cup finely chopped parsley
½ cup finely chopped spearmint
½ cup finely chopped dill
2 tbsp olive oil
½ cup rice
salt, pepper
For the egg-lemon sauce:
2 eggs and 2 lemons

Combine all ingredients in a large bowl and let the mixture stand for 1-2 hours.

Shape the balls and place on floured surface. Put 1,5 liter water in a pot, bring to the boil and drop the meat balls one at a time. Boil them for 20-30 minutes.

Turn off heat and prepare the egg-lemon sauce: Beat egg whites and continue with yolks, lemon juice and a little broth from the pot so that the temperature is balanced. Remove the pot from the heat and stir egg-lemon sauce into it. Add a little salt, if needed.

◁ Meat balls with leeks and spearmint

½ kilo minced meat
2-3 leeks (only the white part)
2 eggs
1 tbsp finely chopped spearmint
1 teaspoon oregano
salt, pepper
1 egg, 1 lemon

Clean leeks, blanch in boiling water for 5 minutes and chop them.

Combine minced meat with the other ingredients.

Heat 3 tbsp olive oil in a pot and sauté meatballs on all sides. Cover with water and cook for 20 minutes. Turn off heat and prepare the egg-lemon sauce as above.

◁ Meatballs with oregano

½ kilo minced meat
½ cup stale bread, soaked in water and squeezed to remove excess water or 2 grated potatoes
2 grated onions
1 egg
2 crashed garlic cloves
2 tbsp olive oil
½ cup grated cheese (optional)
1 tbsp oregano
salt, pepper
2 tbsp vinegar or wine (optional)

For the frying: 2 eggs
1 cup ground toasted bread
1 cup olive oil

Right: Meatballs
with herbs in egg-lemon sauce

Meat balls with oregano

Meat balls with marjoram

Combine minced meat with egg, bread or potatoes, onion, garlic, cheese, oregano, salt and pepper and let the mixture stay in the refrigerator for 2 hours.

Beat 2 eggs in a bowl and put ground toasted bread in another.

Heat olive oil in a frying pan. Shape the meatballs, dip in egg first, then in toasted bread and fry in hot olive oil until brown on all sides. Drain on absorbing paper.

❖ **Variation:** *After frying the meatballs, cover with 2 cups yoghurt and cook in the casserole with 2 tbsp olive oil (Lebanese meatballs).*

⌒ Meatballs with marjoram, parsley and spearmint

As above.

These meatballs are flavoured with 1 teaspoon marjoram, 1 tbsp parsley and 1 tbsp spearmint. Dredge meatballs in flour and fry in olive oil.

⌒ Meatballs with fennel seeds

As above.

Flavour the meatballs with 1 tbsp fennel seeds.

⌒ Minced meat pies with marjoram and thyme

For the pastry dough:
½ kilo flour
1 teaspoon salt
3 tbsp olive oil
1 package dried yeast
½ cup water
½ cup milk

For the filling:
½ kilo minced meat
2-3 tbsp olive oil
1 finely chopped onion

2 finely chopped garlic cloves
½ kilo finely chopped tomatoes
1 tbsp marjoram
1 tbsp thyme
salt, pepper
½ cup grated cheese

Prepare the dough: Dissolve yeast in tepid water, add milk, olive oil, salt and flour, little by little, until the dough is smooth and elastic.

Prepare the filling: Heat olive oil in a saucepan and sauté onion and garlic for 2-3 minutes. Add minced meat and sauté for 10 more minutes.

Pour in tomato, season with salt, pepper and the herbs and cook until the sauce thickens, about half an hour. Turn off heat and stir in cheese.

In the meanwhile the dough has risen. Divide into 8-10 parts and roll out into circles. Put some filling on each one and fold to cover the filling in a moon-like shape. Press the edges to close firmly and place the pies on oiled baking tin.

Let them stand for 10-15 minutes, brush with beaten egg and bake in moderate oven until golden brown, about half an hour.

⤳ Meat pies with lemon balm

As above.
Do not use tomato and, instead of marjoram, use 2 tbsp lemon balm.

BREAD,

⤳ Bread with basil and spearmint

3 cups flour
1 package dried yeast
3 tbsp olive oil
1 cup tepid water
1 tbsp honey or sugar
½ teaspoon salt
2 tbsp finely chopped basil
1 teaspoon oregano
1 teaspoon spearmint

Mix flour with dried yeast, salt, herbs, honey or sugar and olive oil. Add tepid water and knead until the dough is smooth and elastic. Cover with plastic wrap and allow it to rise, until doubled in bulk.
Knead again for a few minutes and shape a round bread or 5-6 smaller breads.
Place on oiled pan, cover and let it rise in a warm place until doubled in bulk again. Brush with beaten egg white and bake in moderate oven until golden brown.

⤳ Bread with sun-dried tomatoes and basil, rosemary or sage

As above.
Add 1 cup sun-dried tomatoes and, if desired, 1 cup olives.

⤳ Cheese bread with calendula petals and thyme

2,5 cups whole wheat flour
1 cup polenta
2 eggs
1 package dried yeast
1 cup milk
or ½ cup milk
and ½ cup water

BISCUITS AND SWEETS WITH HERBS

1 tbsp honey
3 tbsp olive oil
½ teaspoon salt
1 cup grated cheese
(feta, chaloumi or kasseri)
1-2 tbsp calendula petals
1 tbsp thyme

Beat eggs, add yeast diluted in the warm milk, olive oil, honey, water, a little salt, cheese and the flour, little by little, stirring constantly. Finally add the herbs and knead until dough is smooth and elastic.

Cover with a clean towel and let it rise, for about half an hour.

Transfer to a floured surface, punch down, form it into a ball and place in an oiled loaf pan. Cover and allow it to double again.

Paint the surface with beaten egg-white and bake in moderate oven for about 40 minutes.

❧ Cheese bread with lavender and oregano

As above.
Add 2 tbsp lavender flowers and 1 tbsp oregano.

❧ Cheese bread with onion and sage

As above. Add 1 teaspoon dried or 1 tbsp fresh sage.

◆ *You can also use spearmint, dill, parsley, basil or marjoram.*

❧ Focaccia with rosemary and marjoram

3 cups flour
1 package dry yeast
4 tbsp olive oil
1 cup water
2 tbsp honey or sugar
½ teaspoon salt
1 tbsp finely chopped fresh rosemary
1 teaspoon finely chopped marjoram

Dilute yeast, salt and honey or sugar into the warm water. Add 1 tbsp olive oil and flour and knead for 10 minutes until elastic and malleable dough is formed.

Cover with plastic wrap and allow to rise, until doubled in bulk.

Bread with sun-dried tomatoes, basil and rosemary.

Knead again for a few minutes and flatten out into a circle. Place on oiled pan, cover and allow to rise in a warm place until doubled in bulk again. Pestle remaining 3 tbsp olive oil with the herbs and rub the mixture gently into the surface of the focaccia dipping your fingers into a few spots. Sprinkle with a little salt and bake in preheated moderate oven until golden brown.

Fig bread with anise or fennel seeds

½ cup water
½ cup milk
1 package dry yeast
3 tbsp olive oil
1 teaspoon salt
1 egg
3 tbsp sugar
1 teaspoon anise or fennel seeds
2 tbsp ouzo
1 cup dried figs, finely chopped
½ cup coarsely chopped walnuts
½ kilo flour

Dissolve yeast in warm water and milk. Add remaining ingredients and knead smooth and elastic dough. Cover with a clean towel and let it rise for 15 minutes. Knead again, shape the bread, either round or long, and place in an oiled baking pan. Cover and allow it to double again. Brush with beaten egg and bake in preheated moderate oven for about 40 minutes.

Raisin bread with anise or fennel seeds

As above. Use raisins instead of figs.

Lebanese pita-bread with zahtar

1 package dry yeast
1 cup warm water
2 tbsp sugar
1 teaspoon salt
3 cups flour
   3 tbsp olive oil (optional)
For the zahtar:
   1 mashed clove of garlic
   3 tbsp thyme
4 tbsp sesame seeds
4 tbsp olive oil
♦ (You can also use oregano, basil, savory, marjoram, grated lemon zest)

Dissolve yeast, sugar and salt in warm water and add flour until the dough is smooth and elastic.
Cover with a clean towel and leave in a warm place to rise until doubled in bulk. Divide the dough into 10 parts and roll them out into thin circles, 10 cm in diameter. Place on oiled baking tin, cover and allow them to rise again. Paint with the zahtar mixture and bake in moderate heat for 15 minutes.

Bread with rose petals

½ kilo flour
1 cup warm water
1 package active dry yeast
2 tbsp honey
3 eggs
½ teaspoon salt
4 tbsp olive oil
½ cup rose petals
1 tbsp cinnamon powder

Dilute yeast in warm water. Stir in honey, eggs, beaten separately, salt and olive oil. Crush rose petals with cinnamon and add to the mixture. Finally add flour little by little until the dough is smooth and elastic. Cover and let rise until doubled in bulk.
Turn the dough onto a floured surface and shape into 2 balls. Place onto oiled loaf

Right: Fig bread with aniseeds.

pans and cover to allow to rise again until double in size. Brush with beaten egg white and bake in preheated moderate oven for about 50 minutes.

∽ Biscuits with anise or fennel seeds

½ cup olive oil
1 cup sugar
1 tbsp crushed anise or fennel seeds
1 teaspoon bicarbonate of soda
2 teaspoons baking powder
1 cup orange juice or milk
700-750 grams flour
1 cup chopped almonds or walnuts or raisins (optional)

Beat olive oil with sugar and add aniseeds and orange juice with bicarbonate of soda diluted in it. Add flour mixed with baking powder, a little at a time, until dough doesn't stick to the fingers but is still soft. If desired, add nuts or raisins.
Shape oblong loaves, place in oiled baking tin, mark thin slices and bake at moderate heat until golden brown. As soon as they cool down, divide the slices and put back into the oven to toast them.

♦ *With the same dough you can make delicious cookies.*

∽ Bread rings with fennel

½ cup olive oil
1 cup water
½ cup finely chopped fennel
½ teaspoon salt
½ teaspoon pepper (optional)
1 package dry yeast
700 grams flour, approximately

Heat 2-3 tbsp olive oil in a pan and sauté fennel for 3-4 minutes. Then grind in the food processor.

Bread rings with fennel

Bread rings with oregano

Dilute yeast in warm water, add remaining olive oil, salt, pepper and finally flour until dough is soft and malleable.

Cover with a clean towel and leave it in a warm place to rise until doubled in bulk. Shape the dough into rings, place in oiled baking tin, quite apart from each other and allow them to rise again, about ½ hour. Bake in preheated moderate oven for about half hour, until they gain a little colour.

Bread rings with herbs

As above. Instead of fennel, use a mixture of herbs, either fresh or dried, such as parsley, oregano, anise, caraway, basil, dill or fennel. You can also add finely chopped onion or garlic.

Cookies with coriander and caraway

½ cup olive oil or butter
½ teaspoon salt
½ cup milk
1 egg
1 teaspoon crushed coriander seeds
1 teaspoon crushed caraway seeds
1 teaspoon baking powder
½ kilo flour

Mix flour with salt, baking powder, coriander and caraway. Make a hole in the center and pour olive oil or butter and milk. Incorporate the ingredients and knead until the dough is soft but doesn't stick to the hands. Let it rest for 10-15 minutes and then roll it out into a circle 1/4 cm thick. Cut out small circles, paint with beaten egg-white and bake in preheated moderate oven for 15-20 minutes.

Cookies with thyme and rosemary

As above. Substitute the herbs and add ½ cup sugar and 1 tbsp grated lemon rind.

Drop cookies with elder and chocolate

½ cup olive oil or butter
3/4 cup sugar
2 eggs
½ cup milk
2 teaspoons baking powder
200 grams chocolate
1 cup chopped almonds or walnuts
1 cup strong elder tea
3 cups flour

Heat the chocolate with the olive oil or butter for a few minutes, until

Cookies with thyme and rosemary

it melts. Let the mixture cool down and add eggs beaten with the sugar, baking powder diluted in milk, elder tea, almonds or walnuts and finally the flour, beating constantly until all ingredients are well blended.

Take teaspoons of dough and drop, one at a time, on baking tray, on cookie sheet. Bake for 15-20 minutes.

If desired, ice the cookies with confectioner's sugar.

♦ *In the same way you can make cookies with anise hyssop flowers, calendula, lavender, ginger or fennel seeds. You can also leave the chocolate out.*

⌒ Rice cookies with cardamom

1 cup olive oil or butter
1 tbsp sugar
3 egg yolks
1 tbsp ground cardamom
3 cups rice flour
2 tbsp poppy seeds

For the syrup: 1 cup sugar
½ cup water
1 teaspoon rosewater

Boil water with sugar for 5 minutes, turn off heat and pour in rose water.
In a large bowl beat olive oil with sugar and yolks.
Add cardamom, rice flour and the syrup, little by little. Knead until the dough doesn't stick to the hands. Let the dough rest for half an hour and then make the biscuits. Place in oiled baking tin, sprinkle with poppy seeds and bake in preheated moderate oven for 10-15 minutes. They don't need to gain colour.

Left:
Drop cookies with elder and chocolate

⌒ Pancakes with elder flowers

½ cup water or milk
2 eggs beaten separately
½ teaspoon salt
grated zest of 1 lemon
1 cup flour
½ cup elder flowers

1 cup olive oil for frying
icing sugar for sprinkling

Beat yolks with water, salt and zest. Add flour and then the egg whites beaten stiff.
Dip flowers in the batter and fry the pancakes in hot olive oil until brown on both sides.
Place on kitchen roll to remove excess oil and serve the pancakes sprinkled with sugar.

✍ Cake with cherries and sage

1 cup olive oil
3/4 cup sugar
2 eggs
1 cup milk or yoghurt
1 tbsp lemon juice
½ teaspoon bicarbonate of soda
grated zest of 1 lemon
2 tbsp fresh sage leaves, finely chopped
2 cups cherries
3 cups self-raising flour

Beat ingredients in the above order and transfer the mixture into an oiled baking tin. Bake in preheatted moderate oven for about 50 minutes.

✍ Cake with mint syrup

½ cup olive oil
½ cup sugar
5 tbsp cocoa
½ cup milk
2 eggs
½ cup chopped walnuts
2 cups self-raising flour

For the glaze: 1 cup sugar
4 tbsp cocoa
1 cup hot water
4 tbsp mint syrup

Beat olive oil with sugar and add

Yoghurt cake

yolks, cocoa diluted in hot milk, walnuts, flour and finally egg-whites beaten stiff. Empty the mixture into an oiled baking tin and bake in preheated moderate oven for 30-40 minutes.

Dilute sugar and cocoa in hot water, add mint syrup and pour the whole syrup over the cake.

✍ Walnut or almond cake with citrus fruits

12 tbsp chopped walnuts or almonds
6 tbsp semolina flour
6 tbsp ground toasted bread
12 tbsp sugar
12 eggs
1 teaspoon baking powder
1 tbsp cinnamon and clove
1 tbsp grated lemon zest
1 tbsp grated orange zest

For the syrup: 1,5 cup sugar
2 cups water
1 cinnamon stick
the peel of 1 lemon and 1 orange

Mix walnuts with semolina flour, toasted bread, baking powder, cinnamon, clove and zest. Add yolks beaten with the sugar and finally egg-whites beaten stiff.

Empty the mixture into an oiled baking tin and bake in preheated moderate oven. Meanwhile prepare the syrup and pour it over the cake.

❧ Yoghurt cake with lemon and cardamom

1 cup butter or olive oil
1 cup sugar
4 eggs
1 cup yoghurt
the juice of 1 lemon
1 tbsp ground cardamom
1 teaspoon bicarbonate of soda
½ kilo self-rising flour
½ cup chopped walnuts (optional)

Beat olive oil with sugar and continue with yolks, cardamom, yoghurt, bicarbonate of soda diluted in lemon juice, walnuts and flour.
Finally mix carefully with egg whites beaten stiff, transfer the mixture into an oiled baking tin and bake in preheated moderate oven for about 40 minutes.

♦ *You can layer the baking tin with scented pelargonium leaves and, when it cools down, turn the cake upside down. (See the photo below).*

❧ Apple pie with spearmint or lemon balm

½ cup olive oil
3/4 cup sugar
3 eggs
1 teaspoon cinnamon powder
2 tbsp finely chopped

spearmint or lemon balm
½ teaspoon bicarbonate of soda
1 tbsp baking powder
3 cups flour
½ kilo grated apples

In a large bowl beat olive oil with sugar. Add yolks and then flour mixed with baking powder, bicarbonate of soda, spearmint or lemon balm, cinnamon and apples.
Combine well. Finally add egg-whites beaten stiff and combine carefully. Empty the batter in an oiled baking tin and bake in preheated moderate oven for about 50 minutes.

❧ Figs in wine with fennel and aniseeds

½ kilo figs (fresh or dried)
2 cups sweet wine
½ cup grape juice syrup
1 cinnamon stick
5-6 cloves
the peel of ½ lemon
1 teaspoon ground fennel seeds
1 teaspoon ground aniseeds
½ kilo yoghurt or vanilla ice cream
2 tbsp almonds, toasted and chopped

Marinate figs in the wine, cinnamon, cloves, peel, fennel and aniseeds for 5-6 hours. Transfer into a casserole and boil for 5 minutes. Serve the figs after they have cooled down, over yoghurt or ice cream.

Garnish with scented pelargonium leaves and almonds.

◆ *You can also scent with scented-leaved pelargonium or dill.*

ᔐ Dried figs with herbs

Open figs and dry them in the sun. Then join them again with cocktail sticks. Prepare the aromatic dilution: Boil water with bay leaves, fennel, savory and thyme sprigs for 2-3 minutes. Take the herbs out and layer them in a baking tin.

Dip figs in the scented water, take them out and place in the tin over the herbs. Dry the figs in the oven, at low heat and when they cool down, store in jars. Rub fennel seeds on top and cover the jar.

ᔐ "Pasteli" with poppy seeds

"Pasteli" with sesame seeds and honey is a wedding preparation in many Greek areas bearing a symbolic meaning of fertility.
"Pasteli" with poppy seeds is an ancient variation of this sweet, mentioned in ancient writings (Dioscurides).

½ kilo honey
300 grams sesame seeds
200 grams poppy seeds

Toast sesame seeds, grind 100 grams and mix it with the whole seeds.
Heat honey in a pot for 5 minutes and add sesame and poppy seeds, stirring frequently. Boil until the mixture is thick enough (if you drop a teaspoon of mixture into cold water it doesn't spread but remains intact).
Remove from heat and empty the mixture on a flat surface over grease-proof paper, in a layer 1,5-2 cm thick. Cover with grease-proof paper and roll over it with a rolling pin to flatten the surface.
Allow it to cool down and then cut into pieces in the desired shape.
Serve on lemon or bitter orange leaves.

ᔐ "Sraphylarmia" with mustard seeds

1 kilo grapes, firm and crunchy
1 tbsp mustard seeds
2 cups grape-juice syrup

Rinse grapes and pat dry.
Place in jar with layers of scented pelargonium or walnut leaves and mustard seeds and fill with grape juice syrup.
Seal the jar and store in a dark, cool place.

ᔐ Baked apples or pears with lavender

1 kilo apples
1 cup sweet wine
4 tbsp sugar or honey
1 teaspoon cinnamon powder
½ teaspoon clove powder
1 tbsp lavender

◆ *(You can also use grated ginger, cardamom, aniseeds, lemon verbena, grated lemon zest or sage)*

Peel apples or pears, remove seeds and tough parts with the special utensil or cut in two and place in baking tin.
Pour wine over them, sprinkle with cinnamon and clove, aniseeds and sugar or honey and bake in the oven for about 1 hour, wetting them frequently with the juice from the tin.
Transfer the fruit into a platter and continue cooking the juice until it thickens. Pour the sauce over the fruit and decorate with herb

Right: Dried figs with herbs

leaves. Serve with ice cream, yoghurt or soft myzithra cheese.

♦ **Variation:** *You can fill the apples with 1 cup chopped dried fruit, such as figs, plums or raisins and ½ cup nuts (walnuts and almonds), mixed with a little sugar and a little butter.*

☞ Quince jelly with scented-leaved pelargonium

1 kilo quinces
3 cups sugar
2-3 sprigs of scented-leaved pelargonium
the juice of 1 lemon

Wash and peel quinces, remove seeds and cut in quarters. Tie the seeds, the peels and the scented-leaved pelargonium in a clean cloth and put into a casserole with the quinces.
Cover with water (5-6 cups) and boil until they are soft. Strain through a clean cloth and put the juice into the casserole. It should be 3 cups.
Bring it to the boil, add sugar and lemon juice and simmer for 10-15 minutes until the juice thickens, removing the froth from the surface.
Put the jelly in sterilized jars and keep in a cool place for quite a long time.

♦ **Note**: *You can keep the boiled quinces after you have strained them, add as much sugar as their weight and cook the mixture in a casserole until it becomes thick.*
Spread on flat surface, 2 cm thick, and let it cool down.
Cut into pieces of desired shape and decorate with one whole almond on each piece.

Baked apples with lavender.

Jam with mint.

❧ Apple jelly with herbs

As above. Instead of scented-leaved pelargonium, you can use mint, thyme, lemon verbena, rosemary, lavender or rose petals.

❧ Yoghurt jelly with orange or rose petals

2 packages jelly powder
(rose or orange-scented)
½ cup sugar
1 cup finely chopped fruit of your preference
700 grams strained yoghurt
grated zest and juice of 2 oranges
4 tbsp rose liqueur

Put jelly powder, sugar, zest, liqueur and juice and 1 cup water in a pot, stir and bring to the boil. Let it cool down and mix in the food processor with the yoghurt for 2-3 minutes.
Add the fruit and empty into a mould. Put it into the refrigerator to thicken. Turn the jelly upside down onto a platter and decorate with fruit and rose petals or caramelized orange slices.

❧ Fruit and juice jelly with herbs

1 cup orange juice
1 cup strawberry juice
1 cup apple juice
1 cup apple cut into dice
1 cup cherries
1 cup strawberries
5-6 tbsp jelly powder
½ cup finely chopped mint, lemon verbena or lemon balm

Dilute jelly powder in warm orange juice, mix with the rest of the ingredients and empty into a mould. Put in the refrigerator to thicken.

❧ Jam with mint

½ kilo plums
½ kilo apples
800 grams sugar
3-4 mint sprigs

Rinse fruit and pat dry.
Remove seeds from plums, peel the apples and cut into pieces. Put fruit and sugar into a pot and cook until the mixture thickens.
Towards the end add mint and stir constantly so that the jam doesn't stick to the bottom of the pot. Put into sterilized jars and store in a dark cool place.

❧ Lemon marmalade with lemon balm

1 kilo lemons
1 kilo sugar
½ cup water
3 tbsp finely chopped lemon balm

Rinse lemons, pat dry and grate them. Squeeze to remove the juice and mash the pulp.
Put the mashed pulp into a pot with the sugar and let stand for 1-2 hours.
Pour in water, turn on the heat and simmer until the mixture thickens, stirring constantly so that the marmalade doesn't stick to the bottom of the pot.
Add lemon balm and turn off the heat.

❧ Strawberry sweet with elder or lemon verbena

1 layer of sponge cake or biscuits
1 cup strawberry jam

For the custard:
2 cups milk
2 tbsp sugar
2 tbsp vanilla corn flour

Tart with apples and mint.

2 egg yolks
3 tbsp elder flowers or lemon verbena leaves and flowers

Prepare the custard: Boil milk with elder or lemon verbena for 2 minutes after it has come to the boil. Turn off heat and let it stand for 15 minutes.
Strain to remove herbs and put back in the pot with the sugar and the corn flour stirring continuously with the whisk until the mixture thickens. Turn off heat, stir in the yolks and, if desired, 1 tbsp milk butter.
Place a layer of sponge cake or biscuits on a platter and brush with the jam.
Spread the custard over the jam and garnish with strawberries or sprinkle with toasted and chopped almonds.

◆ *You can also flavour the custard with mint or lemon balm.*

✎ Tart with apples or pears and mint

For the pastry dough:
½ cup butter or olive oil
3-4 tbsp sugar
1 egg
3 tbsp mint or other liqueur
1 teaspoon baking powder
2 cups flour

For the filling:
1 kilo apples or pears
1 cup sugar (preferably scented with mint or scented-leaved pelargonium for one week)
2 tbsp finely chopped mint
the juice of 1 lemon
1 cup chopped almonds
4 tbsp liqueur

Myzithra cheese tart with calendula.

Beat olive oil or butter with sugar, continue with beaten egg, liqueur and flour mixed with baking powder and knead until dough is soft and malleable.

Allow the dough to rest for 1 hour.

Grate the apples or pears and boil in a pot with the sugar and the lemon juice until the mixture thickens. Turn off heat and stir in the liqueur and the mint.

Roll out the dough into a circle and layer it on the bottom and the sides of an oiled tart baking tin.

Pierce with a fork on a few spots and cook in preheated oven for 15 minutes.

Spread the jam over the pastry, sprinkle with the almonds and bake for another 40 minutes.

◆ *You can add scented-leaved palargonium instead of mint.*

➣ Myzithra cheese tart with elder or calendula

For the filling:
½ kilo soft myzithra cheese
1 cup strained yoghurt
or ½ cup milk
2 eggs
½ cup sugar or honey
grated zest of 1 orange or pergamot
2-3 tbsp elder or calendula flowers

Prepare the pastry dough as in the previous recipe and layer it on oiled tart tin.

Combine myzithra with yoghurt, grated zest, eggs beaten separately, sugar or honey and elder or calendula petals. Spread the mixture over the pastry, brush with 1 beaten egg and bake in preheated moderate oven for about 50 minutes.

◆ *If desired, put a layer of fruit jelly on top.*

◟ Custard pie with rose petals

3 phyllo sheets
1 liter milk
1 cup rose petals
6 tbsp sugar
6 egg yolks
1 teaspoon rose water

Rinse rose petals, pat dry and crush or rub them with the sugar. Put this mixture and the milk in a pot and bring to the boil. Let it cool down until warm. Add beaten yolks and simmer again until the mixture becomes creamy. Pour in rose water and turn off the heat.

Oil phyllo sheets, one after the other, and layer them on the bottom and sides of an oiled baking tin. Spread custard over the sheets, paint with a beaten egg and bake in preheated moderate oven until the pie gets golden brown.

◆ Variation: *Add half cup semolina flour to the milk for making the custard. You can also flavour with lavender, lemon verbena, spearmint or citrus zest.*

◟ Fruit salad with dried fruit, mint and "myzithra" cheese

1 cup dried figs
1 cup dried pitted prunes
1 cup dried apricots
½ cup raisins
1 cup dates
1 cup sweet wine
1 cup mint tea
grated zest and juice of ½ lemon and ½ orange
2 cups myzithra cheese or ricotta or strained yoghurt
2-3 tbsp honey or grape juice syrup
1 tbsp mint liqueur
½ cup coarsely chopped almonds or walnuts

Put chopped dried fruit, wine, mint tea, lemon and orange zest in a pan and boil for 15 minutes. Let the mixture cool down. Stir in lemon and orange juice and refrigerate for 2-3 hours or more.

In a bowl combine myzithra or yoghurt with liqueur and honey or grape juice syrup. Serve the fruit salad either in a large bowl or in smaller ones topped with 2 tbsp myzithra mixture and garnished with chopped almonds or walnuts and mint leaves.

◆ Variation: *You can also flavour with ground fennel seeds or aniseeds.*

◟ Fruit salad with lavender

1 kilo fruit (peaches, pears, apples, nectarines, bananas, grapes or raisins and pomegranate seeds)
½ cup diced sweet preserve of your preference, with a little from its syrup
2 tbsp liqueur of your desire

grated zest and juice of 1 lemon
1-2 tbsp lavender
½ cup toasted and coarsely chopped almonds

Peel fruit, cut into dice, put in a large salad bowl with the sweet preserve, the syrup, the lavender, the lemon, zest and juice and pour liqueur over them. Stir and refrigerate for 1-2 hours.
Add almonds and garnish with lavender or mint leaves.

⤳ Rose syrup

1 cup rose petals
1 cup water
1,5 cup sugar

Rinse rose petals, pat dry and boil in the water until the sugar melts. Turn off heat, let the syrup cool down, filter it and store in a jar better in the refrigerator.
OR: Pick rose petals every day, put in a jar and sprinkle with sugar (1 tbsp for each rose). When the jar is full, the petals are dried and the sugar has melted. Grind the content of the jar and you will have thick rose syrup.

In the same way you can make **mint syrup** or **scented-leaved pelargonium syrup,** which you can use for flavouring sherbets, tisanes (mostly cold), lemonades and sweets.

⤳ Rice pudding with lemon zest and lemon balm

1 liter milk
½ cup rice
2 cups water
½ cup sugar
grated zest of 1 lemon
1 tbsp finely chopped lemon balm
1 teaspoon cinnamon powder

Boil rice in water for 5 minutes and strain.
Put it back into the pot with the milk, lemon zest, lemon balm and sugar and boil for 15 minutes stirring frequently.
Serve rice pudding in a large bowl or in smaller ones sprinkled with cinnamon and, optionally, with toasted chopped almonds.

*Rice pudding
with lemon zest
and lemon balm.*

❧ Custard with rose water and cardamom

1 liter milk
5 tbsp sugar
3 tbsp corn flour
1 tbsp ground cardamom
½ cup chopped almonds or walnuts

Dissolve corn flour in a little milk and put remaining milk in a pot with the sugar and the cardamom.

Turn on heat and, when milk is warm, stir in the corn flour mixture. Simmer until the mixture becomes creamy stirring continuously.

Add rosewater and turn off heat. Empty into bowls and sprinkle with toasted and chopped almonds or walnuts. Keep in the refrigerator. Garnish with rose petals before you serve.

◆ *You can also flavour with bay leaves, lavender or lemon verbena.*

HERBAL ICED DRINKS

❧ Yogurt and fruit shake with mint

3 cups milk
1 cup strained yoghurt
3 apples, bananas, peaches or pears
3 tbsp sugar
2 tbsp mint

Put mint in the milk and leave it for 1-2 hours. Add remaining ingredients and beat in the mixer until creamy. Refrigerate and serve in glasses garnished with mint leaves.

❧ Milk shake with mint

1 cup milk
½ cup vanilla ice cream
1 tbsp mint liqueur
1 sprig of mint

Combine milk, mint liqueur and ice cream in a blender until creamy.
Pour into a glass and serve immediately with a sprig of mint on top.

❧ Yogurt beverage with lemon balm

2 cups lemon balm tea
2 tbsp honey
1 cup strained yoghurt

Combine all ingredients in a blender. Serve over ice cubes.

☙ Iced lemon verbena tea with apple or peach juice

2 cups lemon verbena tea
1 cup apple juice
2 tbsp sugar

Make the tea, add sugar and, after it has
cooled down, mix with the juice. Serve over
ice cubes and decorate with lemon verbena
leaves.

❖ **Variation**: *Instead of apple, you can use
peach or grape juice. You can also add dried
apple peel.*
❖ *Instead of lemon verbena, you can use rose
petals, lemon balm or elder flowers.*

☙ Iced mint tea

Iced mint tea is a wonderful treat.
Put 2 tbsp mint leaves in 2 cups boiling water
and steep for 10 minutes. Filter, let the tea
cool down and serve with ice cubes and a
mint leaf in each glass.

Lemonade with lemon verbena.

♦ *You can also add a little mint liqueur or mint syrup.*

⊱ Grape sherbet with mint

1 cup water
1 tbsp mint
1 cup grape juice

Bring water to the boil, transfer into a teapot, add mint, cover and steep until it cools down. Serve on ice cubes, preferably scented with mint.

♦ **Variation**: *Use scented-leaved pelargonium or lavender instead of mint. Similarly you can make sherbet with strawberries, peaches, sour cherries or apricots.*

⊱ Orange sherbet with lavender

1 cup orange juice
1 tbsp sugar
1 tbsp lavender flowers

Put sugar, juice and lavender in a pot and boil until the sugar melts, stirring frequently. Allow the juice to cool down and then put in the freezer. When it starts to freeze, take it out and beat in the mixer. Put in the freezer again. Shortly before serving, take it out of the freezer, let it defrost lightly and beat again in the mixer. Serve the sherbet in glasses garnished with herb leaves.

⊱ Lemonade with lemon balm or lemon verbena

1 liter water
½ cup lemon juice
½ cup sugar
3 tbsp minced lemon balm
or lemon verbena

Combine all ingredients in a bowl and chill for at least 2-3 hours. Strain out the leaves and serve in glasses over ice cubes.
Decorate with a lemon balm or lemon verbena leaf on top.

✺ Fruit juice with elder flowers

1 apple, 1 orange
1 kiwi, 1 peach
4 tbsp sugar
2 tbsp lemon juice
½ cup elder flowers

Peel and mash the fruit. Add sugar, lemon juice and elder flowers and refrigerate for a few hours. Filter and serve in glasses with elder flowers on top.

◆**Variation:** *You can also flavour the juice with mint, lemon balm or lavender.*

HERB INDEX
(COMMON NAMES)

HERB INDEX
(SCIENTIFIC NAMES)

INDEX OF RECIPES

SELECTED BIBLIOGRAPHY

♦ BOTANICAL:
IETSWARRT, J.,H., 1980: A taxonomy revision of the genus Origanum, Leiden Univ. Press.
KAVVADAS, D., 1956: Βοτανικό φυτολογικό λεξικόν, v. 1-9, Athens.
KOKKINI S., 1993: Έκθεση αποτελεσμάτων ερευνητικού προγράμματος φαρμακευτικών φυτών Κρήτης-Ηπείρου.
MESSAEGUE, M., 1983: Υγεία και ζωή, translated by L. Kypraeou.
SCHAUENBERG P., & PARIS, F., 1977: Guide medicinales, Neuchatel-Paris.
TUTIN T.G. et al. (Eds), 1964-1993: Flora Europaea Vols 1-4 First edition, Vol 1 second edition, Cambridge University Press.
WALLIS T.E., 1946: Textbook of Pharmacognosy, London.
GENNADIOS P., 1959: Λεξικόν Φυτολογικόν v. 1-2, Athens.
SKOUBRIS B., 1985: Αρωματικά-Φαρμακευτικά φυτά, αιθέρια έλαια, Salonica.
FRANGAKI E., 1969: Συμβολή εις την δημώδη ορολογίαν των φυτών, Athens.

♦ GENERAL:
AEKATERINIDIS G., 1973: Λαϊκή ιατρική (18th c.), Athens.
Apostolidis P., 1997: Ερμηνευτικό λεξικό πασών των λέξεων του Ιπποκράτους, Athens.
GALANOS D., 1984: Θέματα Χημείας τροφίμων, Αθήνα.
EMMANOUEL EMM., 1934: Η φαρμακοποιία δια μέσου των αιώνων, Athens.
EUTICHIADIS AR., 1983: Εισαγωγή εις την Βυζαντινήν θεραπευτικήν, Athens.
KYPRIANOU TH., 2000: Από τη χλωρίδα της Κύπρου, Leukosia, Cyprus.
MPIMPI - PAPASPYROPOULOU A., 1985: Παραδοσιακή ιατρική στην Πελοπόννησο, Athens.
PAPAVASILIOU J. - ROZOS P., 1979: Εγχειρίδιον Ιστορίας της Ιατρικής, Athens.
PAPADAKIS MILT., 1976: Μορφαί του λαϊκού πολιτισμού της Κρήτης του 15ου και 16ου αι., Athens.
PAPADOGIANNAKIS N. (ed.), 2001: Κρητικό ιατροσόφιον του 19ου αι., Rethymnon.
PLATAKIS EL., 1975: Ο δίκταμος της Κρήτης, Heraklion.
ROUTSETAKIS EL., 1939-40: «Γιατροσόφια», mag. Δρήρος, v. 3.
PSILAKIS N., 1996: Κρητική Μυθολογία, Heraklion.

♦ ANCIENT AND BYZANTINE:
AGAPIOS: Αγαπίου Μοναχού του Κρητός, Γεωπονικόν, Βενετία. ed D. Kostoulas, Volos.
AETIUS: By Alex. Olivetti, ed. Teubner, 1950.
ATHENAEUS: LOEB Classical Library, London 1927–1941.
CASSIANUS VASSUS: Cassiani Bassi, Geoponica, De re rustica eclogae, Recensuit Henricus Beckh, Lipsiae 1895.
GALENUS: By D.C.G. Kuhn, Lipsiae 1821-1833.
DIOSCURIDES: ed. Max Wellman, Berlin 1906.
HIPPOCRATES: Ed. the Loeb Classical Library, 1923-1995, London.
OREIBASIUS: Migne J. P. Patrologia Graeca, v. 103.
PAULUS AEGINITA: By I. L. Heberg, ed. Teubner, 1921.